49th PARALLEL PSALM

49th PARALLEL
P S A L M

■ ■ ■

WAYDE COMPTON

ADVANCE EDITIONS
Vancouver

49TH PARALLEL PSALM
Copyright © 1999 by Wayde Compton
Second Printing: 2005

ADVANCE EDITIONS
an imprint of
ARSENAL PULP PRESS
103-1014 Homer Street
Vancouver, B.C. Canada V6B 2W9
www.arsenalpulp.com

The publisher gratefully acknowledges the support of the
Canada Council for the Arts and the B.C. Arts Council for its
publishing program.

Canadä

The publisher gratefully acknowledges the support of the
Government of Canada through the Book Publishing Industry
Development Program for its publishing activities.

Typeset by the Vancouver Desktop Publishing Centre
Printed and bound in Canada

CANADIAN CATALOGUING IN PUBLICATION DATA:
Compton, Wayde, 1972-
49th parallel psalm

Poems.
ISBN 1-55152-065-6

1. Black-Canadians—History—19th century—Poetry.*
2. Afro-Americans—Migrations—History—19th century—
Poetry. I. Title.
PS8555.O5186F6 1999   C811'.54   C99-910361-X
PR9199.3.C65F6 1999

CONTENTS

ACKNOWLEDGEMENTS

For my mother and father, Patricia and Levi Compton.

Respect to:
The Black Cultural Association, George Bowering, the Canada Council, George Elliott Clarke, the Comptons (Shawn, Sylvia, Alisha, Tyson), Marilyn Dumont, Paul Dutton, Karen Earl, Cynthia Flood, Isabel Flood, Nancy Gillespie, David Gutteridge, Michael Hewitt, Athena Hilts, Wendy Hilts, Carissa Holmes, Peter Hudson, Jeet Kei Leung, Reg Johanson, Dan Kashagama, Susan Kauffmann, Angela Kayira, Donna Kilgallin, Ryan Knighton, Blaine Kyllo, Brian Lam, Jason Le Heup, Leo McKay, Roy Miki, Melinda Mollineaux, Tracy Rawa, Vanessa Richards, Vanessa Rockel, Roots of Resistance, George Stanley, Itrath Syed, Third World Alliance, Trevor Thompson, Chris Turnbull, Michael Turner, Karina Vernon, Jan Wade, John Whatley, and the loas who arose.

In memory of Emery Barnes, 1929-1998, and Kwame Toure (Stokely Carmichael), 1941-1998.

Some of these poems first appeared in working form, in the following: *absinthe, Capilano Review, Judy, Kola, Prism international, rout/e, Tads, West Coast Line,* and *Westword.*

CAST

Was it stories first and then people, or the other way round?
—Chinua Achebe

MC

conductor, conductor,
this is over
ture. I sure
foot halfstep
to drums splayed for you. does rum

conduct electricity? drop a dram
on the ground to be grounded,
to be landed,
so we can dig the sound
of the switches and the channels.
Shango flows into the amp.
the tubes warm up.
the filaments erupt.

go fourth and multiply,
go north and fly
to each cardinal point,
and us just
the forth generation from slavery.

conductor, conductor,
ten-four, that's a copy.
multiples of multitudes
on the move
conducive to
a 't'
't' for two
worlds. swallow these spirits I stoke for you.
this mess of embers I am left with.

dancing from one drink
to the next—my god

what have we come to?—my loa
raises a cup of flames to the chaos.
my trick stirrer trips on slurs
and stut

ters: 'my name
is Legba
and I am
an alcoholic.' a swig here
there a sip
and I pick
up
your feed. trans

mission
live on location. I vocalize
how dry I've been. I preen
in my top hat, walking stick,
and afro sheen. live and direct
I push up the levels
on this worn mixing board. treble
and strife. bass
and superstructure. material
and spirit worlds,
dig it—

no rain
gonna wash away
the tracks we layin
down
tonight

SAM

Baron Samedi slaps down
the cover—seven dollars—and shedding
his skin, flicks
one more to the coat-check girl,
sails on in

straight for the gin, mouth bone-dry, thin,
as the tender serves with his left hand
(sloe on the rocks with a tonic Charybdis
and a quicklime twist). the spook
of the eternal blues mouths, 'down the hatch'
through a lipless grin

and steps to the floor.
ghost feet don't glide but skank
like chains or canes
on planks. hearing through the holes
in his head, silent Sam's bones
clatter and sync
opate to the reverb and wine, the grind
of a deck's worth of losing hands. Sam

struts among youth vampirical,
so cool, cooler than miracles.
walking on ice. he
laughs in his top hat at sacrilege. he
scoffs at reluctance to avarice. he
howls. he
counts. he
boogies down,
down in his dusty tux, tails,
and browless frown.
the right Baron Samedi,

perpetually diggin the sound
amongst those with eyes closed in dance
as the strobes *knock knock* on their lids
like ice picks. Sam has a way
of prying his way in. his clearance
is majestic; noble his appearance. regal
is his wriggle; his shimmy and his shackle.
his cough and his sputter; his hack
and your circumstance. dancing,

eyes shut tight. flipping
coins into the cup
of trembling. guessing
on heads or tails or t
cells. taking a path
this way or that. vein
or artery. fading flush of spades
or dead man's hand. Sam

taps, drums, rolls
his bone digits a
cross shoulders to go
as in a child's game of seven up:
heads down.
eyes closed.
dancing slow.
so cold.
so close.
barren Sam
laughs your luck
as Samedi
this time
simply
passes
fastly.

O

O Osiris, rise up.
raise us. some say
you are the original
Christ. some say
Isis, your sister, renewed you
and knew you
in an obscene way. twice

Set, your nemesis (your set),
iced you. the first time
you just rose right on up like the sun.
so the second time the nigger got mean, cut you up
like a DJ would a groove, splintered you like a busted mirror,
razored you good, then spread

the pieces around like a drunk does money
on a Saturday night. buried a piece in the east,
a portion in the north, an ounce in the south,
and the rest in the west. to the four corners, as they say,
he fixed your wagon. but he didn't count

on Isis, cool Isis, who loved you right (wrong)
and sought you out and dug you up. pick and spade
and all. gathered your remains
in a bloody dirty pile and watched the magic work
as you got it together. she shuffled you back to osirisness
like you was a deck. and you stood up again
at last, shook your head, cussed out
that punk motherfucker Set, gave Isis a big wet kiss,
and asked her to fill you in
on what had gone down. and after she did, you said,

'the only question I got, sis, is
if he burried a part of me in the west, which,
as all of us Egyptians know, is where heaven lies,
what was heaven like?' and Isis replied

'Osiris, bro, how else would heaven be?
it was blue.'

'just blue? that's all?'

'you forget to put on your ears? I said it was blue.
all sorts of blue.'

JD

*the first governor of the colonies of British Columbia and Vancouver's
Island. the Chief Factor of the Hudson's Bay Company on the west coast.
spring of 1858 he encouraged blacks from California to come north, just
in time to fill the labour shortage in B.C. the gold rush was about to
cause. he coolly withdrew support for them upon their arrival.*

*father Scottish, mother from British Guyana, he never confirmed nor
denied the rumour that he was part.*

O James Douglas,
our own quadroon Moses,
should I place a violet on your grave
or hawk a little spit
for your betraying ways?
O white man, black when out

of favour. our fates braided
like rutting snakes. the cabal
that is *négritude*. the counter
conspiracy
to make a black northwest be. O

James Douglas,
you held the keys
like a lesser Legba—laughing, shuffling passports,
passing
in your black and white
archival stance. decked nonetheless
in what I dream as Garvey-like imperial plumage. company

man. on the winning team.
backing the right horse. the best telegony.
one thousand eight hundred and fifty-eight years from Christ.
in the wilderness. far from home
and the Caribbean
and ancient Rome. Britannia rules
the roost
and waves
a few
blacks on through
from slavery to

the freedom to be
loyal man
power for a crown expansion. man
acled to the company town
and second-hand scansion.

O James Douglas,
did you ever see yourself
in us?
did you ever stop
in your war versus the wilderness
and think

we?

EX

prayer:
microphone become dumb,
stand turn to Damballah,
wire into weir. wail
for the sinkers,
the swimmers,
and those who walked all the way home
on a road of starfish, barnacles, shells,
and drier promises.

a backwards prophecy

wanders at Ambleside Beach,
North Shore, in the foothills.
treading, buoyant
and tricked. tangle-eyed, scroll-lipped.
wrapped
in rags
bluely
doomed. shuffling through
the comet's tail of our time's
boom
for spare stray silver schooners, queens, cariboo.
hands scooped
for a share. he washes
his dreaded silvered hair
of dreams
in the drinking

fountain. sifts
the sand for coins with his drift
wood cane. looking for cans. his cane engaged
in a kind

of cuneiform. signaturing the breach
at Ambleside. the bank. the brink. the far
side of fair. his eyes comb

the tines of the Narrows, the Lion's Gate
Bridge. squints the shores together. hintered in
to Zion's hate. stones in the sole
of his wholeness. sandles running over
with sand. his gravelled barritone.
his flot
sam cane
of jet
sam drift
wood
worn
like bone.
cane tracing
the shore like the finger of none
other
than god. the tide

wanders home, mumbles a
part his scat
soliloquy. his scat
tered cipher.
his nonunmeaningless meandering
in
cant
ations
as he, worn wordless, walks
into the in
let for his Is

rael . . .

NO

when the berries rot
>   and
>   fall and ferment
on the soft
>   urn of earth, the bohemian waxwings
kern
>   and wing
>   down, turn

whistling
>   their words
tween up and down.
>   they land
on their forgot
>   ten feet, then lap
at the ripest,
>   ripest
>   whirl.

>   and drunk,

the birds flap _____

up

        up to

sleep it

    off on

        a bed of blue.

and like Noah,
        do they too
have to get again used to
           their element?
    do they too
feel their joints
    buckling?
        do they too
    earn a seven-coloured covenant
        maybe painted on the grass
by their maker
      in blessed
    and crushed
berry

    blood?

DJ

stimulator of the inner simulacra
                              turner of the worlds
lobe and hip at one with the word
                              conduit of the herd
shepherd of the unheard
                    hands on the vinyl
needle in the curve
                turntable arm prosthetic
phantom limb pinning down the intersections—

jungle and house   soul and techno   euro and rhythm and blues

cues the anticipation
                    plays our feet and strums our blood
alcohol permeates the paradigmatic
                              digs his fingers into static
crossfades the synth with beaten blood
                                   like a clock of tactic
turns the syntagmatic backwards
                         scratches 'bring that beat back'
catches
        the loop on the off
beat   matches
                that per minute mix like magic
makes the walls shake and the bass roll dashes
                                   your soul
against the table's glasses
                    the waitress passes

on the next round she wades in
delivers sapphires of liqueur
under black light
gets our orders all wrong

we pass and swivel and change chairs
to put the drinks wrongside right
the waitress wades back through the bass   the mix
the sound's humidity
the tindery contagion of humanity and electricity
touching touching
and she's gone

a hand on the texts and tomes   the keeper
spins limbs   the griot
holds in his collection the keys to corporeal
wisdom   this body of texts
these twelve-inch tablets of counterclockwiseness   the old
school warmth of vinyl and tubes   the blues
in the hyperbolic hip hop and trickster electronica
more singles in the crates than scrolls in the ancient library
of Alexandria

castanets
from hinges
snare drum
from this splintered jamb
bass from pane
we kick the damn
door down   chant
from chastisement
sticks
from names that wound
like a clock past tense wound
recyclers
scavengers
swallowers
excreters
of sound
dip
the divine stylus   drop

the needle
flip
through files
for the right disc   switch
the crossfader to the left side
snare
knock knocking   lift
the right
drop it   drop
the needle on the next
cut cutting
rock
knock knock knocking
Papa   Labas
open the doors
straddle the roles
dip   your oar
of ear
or ear
d'or
pan west
then north
then on   and on
back backwards and back to back
ear we are
ear for or
rockin in
our fly new gear
our hype blue camouflage

THEIR

I met History once, but he ain't recognize me.
—Derek Walcott

San Francisco: 1858

RECORDS

here we're

the ful
crum of for
tune, backs halved
like rusted hasps. train hands. sweat oiling
tracks,
switches,
tension,
sinew,
axels in the clock's unending 'got to.' shoe-

shiners, boot-
makers, doom-
mestics, ticket-
takers, white-baby-
raisers, tear-
tasters: we

're the ones that made it
here, got it to
gether just as much as any
body here.
where even eyeballing the horizon'll
get you pegged as uppity. gotta watch your
self. the free

Negroes of San Francisco, 'hallelujah'
in each sun-assaulted hand, raying like one
lodestar among
multitudes: a harvest of digits
testifying. in church. in Zion
Church. voicing

our minds. our voices
turn over. tilled. in the leg

islature, whites, teeth-like,
argue us over. how alive we are.
on pages brand names. mouths
one 'hear!hear!' ahead
of making the west the south.

—a north star wish—

please pull us some levers,
maybe
deus ex us outta here
cause I hear
the black train of death.
it's grinding on wheels of steel
like the gnashing of teeth.

grandmother, high golden,
hands like supplicating spiders,
works the work. boils on the front burner; curses
on the back. simmers in her pot
slavers' names—*Smiths*, *Joneses*—owning names. picks a
part the entrails of a compass, pins the points of pain
to wax figure faces.

—ain't blues—

ain't got no ballot,
ain't got no flintlock,
ain't got no cannon,
ain't got no big talk.
ain't got nothin
but a mouth fulla ain't got.

by a combination of mother wit
and constellation literacy, arrived. got
t work harder. got
t be smarter. got
t runner farther jus
t stand still.

—polisher's holler—

(spit) shine, (spit) shine
one thin dime for Frisco's best.
(spit) shine, (spit) shine
one thin dime for Frisco's best.
(spit) shine, (spit) shine

(while California's still the west).

first black newspaper in California.

we read be
tween. we be
lieve be
tween. we
be be
tween

the lines.

The Mirror of the Times
səmiT ɘht ʇo ɹoɿɿiM ɘhT

smell of seeping ink and print, we push some slim mannequin of truth into
the slow howl of these machines that spin out words on wheels. we turn.
wind, like watches. spin like mills. this eddy in the deathly stream of
Virginian indigo.

> *stop the presses!* we holler. one more story dances under the dead
> line.

front page headline boldface prose blues in black ink, correcting the spaces.
our living breathing in-God's-image bodies and souls rendered a kind of
King James typo. cut, seared, and wealed. we peel sheet from sheet. as thin
as this. and when I finish a day's work, my white palms are as black as the
backs of my hands. the ink smells its own kind of clean. I broke this story
myself. got the scoop at bawling age. put it under births and deaths: Born

`under a bad sign; been down since I began to`
`crawl`. paging stories carefully carefully, cleaving the truth from the woe of these halting chalky syllables. this blank murk in which I must express weself. we Negroes 'of letters,' as they say. as we press into papyrus. as we scroll and scribe. as we spit into the wind of history, to be swallowed, rained, and reswallowed. this blur of cruel serifs at the gate swinging swords, editing us from Eden, us from Africa, us from us. as we go to press, late breaking,

Narcissus reclaimed as Ethiopian; Ovid to testify in 'Swarthygate' scandal

this English, this snare of erudition, imported thorns to the tongue. these keys, these cutting punches, feel like prosthetic eyes. blocking. my. view. the times. my tongue. my byline. the aching cant. this labyrinth. the typeset. the moveable. nothing but moveable. all we got is moveable. the way the wind blows. my hands at the end of the day. all I got. not even my letters. a Negro 'of letters.' a 'Negro' of letters. uppity and inbetween the lines. black to black, stained and steeped, like those of us still captured in indigo 'down home,' as we say. reaching for a piece. a wave. to make. something. indelible.

when I touch the sails of white newsprint, forgetting myself, my hand says,

HABEAS CORPUS

xxxxxxxxxxxxxxxxxxxxxxxxxxxxxxxxxxxxxxxxxxxxxxxxxxxxxxxxxxxxxxx

—1848
the public schools are segregated the way a book opens the way a book
closes h in ges we build our own in stitutions or go with—

xxxxxxxxxxxxxxxxxxxxxxxxxxxxxxxxxxxxxxxxxxxxxxxxxxxxxxxxxxxxxxx

—The Civil Practises Act of 1850
is passed. degraded and demoralized blacks from
Africa, Indians from Patagonia, South Sea
Islanders, Hawaiians, Chinese and other peoples
of color can no longer testify in court against whites. can I get a—

xxxxxxxxxxxxxxxxxxxxxxxxxxxxxxxxxxxxxxxxxxxxxxxxxxxxxxxxxxxxxxx

—The Fugitive Slave Act of 1852
to catch. the desire to purge the State of this class
of inhabitants, who, in the language of a
distinguished jurist, are 'festering sores upon
the body politic,' entered largely into the
consideration of the Leg—

xxxxxxxxxxxxxxxxxxxxxxxxxxxxxxxxxxxxxxxxxxxxxxxxxxxxxxxxxxxxxxx

—The Poll Tax of 1857
blacks must pay a tax on the vow though blacks can't X. a tax—

xx

—1858 Bill 339
is finally proposed to restrict and prevent the
immigration to and residence in the state of
negroes and mulattoes, closing

the west. / stretched / forth fingers touch / *The Mirror*'s words: 339. / to be
cut / off from ones / home / down. / the ink runs / and so the others / mired
in numbers. / the running ones, the family members / cut off from / the free
edge of the sun. / setting / typing / blood / on that congealing body of—

JUMP ROPE RHYME OF THE 49ER DAUGHTERS

caller got a treasure map and a silver pick.
all how you gonna know where to dig?

caller map got a great big X on it.
all how you gonna know where to dig?

caller got 10 paces marked in black.
all how gonna know where to dig?

caller gonna count em off . . .
all 1, 2, 3, 4, 5—gonna count em off.

caller gonna count em off . . .
all 6, 7, 8, 9, 10—gonna count em off.

caller gonna count em off . . .
all 1, 2, 3, 4, 5—gonna count em off.

caller gonna start again . . .
all 6, 7, 8, 9, 10—gonna start again.

caller got a treasure map with a silver spade.
all how you gonna know where to dig?

caller just like a pirate with a wooden leg.
all how you gonna know where to dig?

caller girl in the middle gotta spell her name . . .
all how you gonna know where to dig?

caller jumpin on one foot, okay?
all jumpin on just one foot.

girl A-l-e-x-a-n-d-r-i-a.
all how you gonna know where to dig?

CRUCIAL BLUES

can't seem

to discern if the scent of the sea is pure
or rank. it's red
tide, and I'm
sittin on the dock
wastin time
prophesying. in court, on the dock, these days
wastin time
trying to prepare a path through the Latin,
the reign. this time
of decision. these days
of gathering
stones together. we congre
gate at Zion

Church. strike
a Pioneer Committee
like lightning might slice
a key from night. at
Zion Church,
Babel's harbour, my hands dip in
to my pockets like oars. I reach for
change. my do
nation. I view the weathered expressions
cupped in hands, or hands in over
all pockets, or folded like
documents: all some
how recalcitrant
in lamentation. the race

man from Philly
is running down the topography
of our hope. it's proposed
the Pioneer Committee will un
earth us some new some
where: settlement, sediment, coast. I notice
no one uses the word *home*.

the Pioneer Committee is set to lo
cate some *terra in*
cognita in the inlet
of our tears, to shovel us like coal in
to a steamer, tack our
selves in waves. the ones
tired of dreaming, being
streamed in
to teams of tiers and spun
like weary wheels
of legality.
a map is spread a
cross our hope:
rivers, tendrils, veins, and holms.
we read the legend, measure out our
prospects, our
exodus, our
chances, our
choices:

Panama,

Sonora,

Vancouver's Island.

THE CHIEF FACTOR

If the majority of immigrants be American, there will always be a hankering in their minds after annexation to the United States . . . . They will never cordially submit to English rule, nor possess the loyal feelings of British subjects . . . . The floating population of this Colony have, with very few exceptions, wandered off to the newly discovered gold diggings at Thompson's River, and there will therefore be great difficulty, unless the mines prove a failure, in engaging local white labour.
      —James Douglas to the Colonial Office in London, spring 1858

of the HBC,
a funnel
to our pour,

blood
to the gears
of here
and labour
and/ore.

blood
of love
or money,
queen
and country: sub
jectivity.

the Chief Factor
drafts
a letter
his signature sings
a lateral quatrain—

lo: there's land north, British,
and literally setting foot
on its soil = citizenship, freedom,
safe quarter exchanged for toil.

DOUGLAS'S COVENANT

I   land can be purchased for I pound per acre.

II   a minimum XXV percent down payment on land is required.

III   the balance on the down payment must be settled in IV yearly installments.

IV   the down payment will run at V percent interest.

V   land will not be taxed until MDCCCLX.

VI   holding land for IX months earns one the right to vote and sit on juries.

VII   after residing in the colony for VII years, one may take an oath to the Crown

and become subject.

THE COMMODORE

Whereas, We are fully convinced that the continued aim of the spirit and policy of our mother country, is to oppress, degrade and outrage us. We have therefore determined to seek asylum in the land of strangers from the oppression, prejudice and relentless persecution that have pursued us for more than two centuries in this our mother country. Therefore a delegation having been sent to Vancouver's Island, a place which has unfolded to us in our darkest hour, the prospect of a bright future; to this place of British possession, the delegation having ascertained and reported the condition, character, and its social and political privileges and its living resources.

—from a statement composed by members of San Francisco's black community at Zion Church, 1858

from Pacific and Folsom Wharf
in SF
thirty-five left
full of fathoming
on the run
the San Francisco-Victoria run
in the hold
afloat
and hovering
over the hull and ahoy
in limbo
baleful
on deck under the night's moon
ahoy
over
board
the ribs creaking
avast

under cover
of darkness
the steamer *The Commodore*
carries
thirty-five black arrivants
aimed
at the colony
of Vancouver's Island
and I
over
the railing deliver
my interior to the sea
my inward debt
my survivor's agony
of dreams
my soul spins
I step
on deck
but my feet
miss the rhythm
I steal to the hold
my room full of mirrors
my huddled brothers
our Pioneer Committee
vomitting from the depths
of our ancestry
no one sleeps

the steamer *The Commodore*
under
the thin thunder
of April timbre
I wonder where
will this endeavor
let us land
I wonder how

our blues
will rhyme with Vancouver
I wonder what
we'll have to sew
to scythe some sovereignty
I count our meagre numbers
on fingers
on fringes
on prostheses of clay

to by to
forty mays
and forty mights
counting leagues
as the dreams roll by
white caps
fathoming
our segue
tide
beside
white men
Americans
gold rushers
feverish
for the coast
counting leagues
I lean
against the rail
for a sign
I see
the rise
of an island
Vancouver's Island
our colony
fore of the bow

XANADA

When you lose you become ancient
—Dionne Brand

BERTH PRAYER

*On Sunday Apl. 25 the Commodore Capt. Nagle, arrived with 400 or
500 Emigrants from San Francisco . . . . There were also 35 men of
colour from the same place of different trades and callings, chiefly
intending to settle here. On Monday (Apl. 26) drinking tea at Mrs.
Blinkhorn's with my wife she (Mrs. B) told us that on the precedg evening
she was surprised at hearing the sounds of praise. They proceeded from
the men of colour who had taken a large room at Laing's the Carpenter;
& they spent the Sabbath Evening in worshipping the word of God.*

—Reverend Edward Cridge, from his diary

sea-legs, go
          from me;
let
                    my step
find the beat
          of the dirt.

nausea, reeling, relent; we are at
last
sent.

wearily we'll steel ourselves
and weigh, like an anchor,

new roots,
rhythm,

earth
     back in
earth.   sea-legs,

listen. my song
is an answer, an imperative am
putation.

       listen.

COMPANY

this land
        is the company's own
ed, paid for. I wander it.
prospecting, guessing, divining ground. counting
days till
this transforms to home. in

my holy ghostly breath, I whisper fissured worksongs in
to hollowness. songs like the bones of eagles' wings under
cutting some corner of blue. wings
like spades cutting. under
wind and blue. in the in
terior, prospecting, guessing, cutting, carrying
pieces back to Victoria where
wood clapped

together makes side
walks, creaking, sounding
like scars. my boots cracking
in the half-made streets, tacking
from saloon to general store, mud caking,
British Columbia itself flushed, hardening,
shaping. they call

the HBC cash 'script.' you can ex
change it for bottled destiny. ships in
side or sin
sold by the shot. bottle of hot
white
gin. bottle that could be chopped, used
for slide   guitar. turned
to wailing. but ain't. I

just shuffle on in
to the in
terior again, an emptier of earth, shovelling,
this my dusty hustle, a dirt rustler. three cards face
down, I shuffle
script for bread, breath, heart, preciousness.
gold an earth bone ex
posed. I, the sluice
shaker, the cash-maker. chasing
money money pounds almighty. singin, workin, spinnin
a silver pan at the river's shoulder—

> good great God Lord, give me strength
> to take another stone up from the well of stones.
> good great God Lord give me strength
> to take my heart on home someday.

panning, like a fool, for Pangaea. hymning—

> church on Sunday, next to the white folks.
> canon-shaped choruses, Anglican-cold.
> church on Sunday, nuggets of wisdom.
> church on Sunday, niggers of gold.

my mind reaches, wishing
for the wailing of a preacher
to bring me. to make me be
lieve, to amen in
to Psalm 137. every

time I hear the word or
take a rock out of this here
heaven, I cave. break. down in
to tears to hear some
familiar speeching. every
time I hear the word nearly

perching me. every
time I hear the word, and in
side the word, gold

or

honey

from the rock. like the word
made flesh. like A
dam and Eve peopling. multiplying.
calling one down. and if she carrying
low, a girl. names over
flowing. like a walking
song—

Camarilla Indigo Ellie Amaranth Epiphany Apocrypha Peripeteia Smith.

simply
seeking nothing but some un
picked-over dreams; a seat in the pew,
if not in the front, not in the back. a psalm
or two. and if the preacher is with
out soul, we'll
hum to the creak of the floor boards. sync
opate it in our minds. tap our feet at least. us, the shufflers

of dust. a sister beats
the rugs of others' houses
for a living. dashing. dashing. we,
a people of the dash. and I,
my church,
founded on the dashing stones. whichever

pieces make it through the sluice gates shining
enough
to gather and wash and sell and melt and mould
enough
to trade for tokens or trinkets or tickets to take us
someday
good great
God Lord
all the way back where we came from.

CLAIMING

lift earth from earth. wring
wealth from dearth. clay
to dust. stones from blood. slashes

to slashes. we
are bandits. brigands
of sand. when the cash
comes to rest
and the sediment
is spent,
we'll commit
to more profitable climes:
partition. divide. mine.
fingers in the earth, holding
like roots.
fingers finger the routes
of the rush,
the flush
of fever,
the viral
entropy of luck,
the flecks
of yellow
I never before noticed
in my own eyes
as I
lean into the silver
of the river.

I

am at the apocalypse of my prospects
when my tongue touches the Fraser's termoil,
hands cupped, lifting the river
to my lips.
I'll never see the veins on the backs of my hands in the same way again.

enough gold lies below
to bribe sight back to the blind.
there are hard rivers
of difficult glitter, betterment
I want
so bad
my sweat
runs cold. we camp, bed
under a smouldering moon. in

deep. a circle of out
casts. Irish, Americans, Chinese, criminals, and one
runaway me. we
are hunters of the hunger
for gold. we
walk sorting thoughts of earth ex
ploding. we
shuffle face cards without laughter. we
will always ever after
sleep with one eye on the trigger
of our trust. we

are in In
dian country. pounding
punctuation, lassoing and staving
our names. bitten by the sight
of stars, the night
with ten thousand teeth takes its tax

of blood. we tend
a fire, sleep,
a shivering coil a
round the smoke's curling cataclasis.
the back of my hand is my pillow. tomorrow
we will axe at the earth's en
trails. but tonight, easy sleep
is all I want out of the dark

in this time
of casting away stones
and of gathering stones together.

'GOD SAVE THE QUEEN' FRAGMENT

                          rise
o Lord our God a
scatter our en
                    e
          mies
and
make
them
fall

confound their politics
frustrate their knavish tricks
on thee our hopes
we fi
          x

o

save us all

NUMBERS: ROMANS

1 counter to Douglas's fairy stories, franchise in the colony was exclusive to British subjects, and only those with property. naturalized subjects faced a court of revision. eighteen blacks who voted in 1860 had their votes discounted, the only voters whose X's were X'ed out.

2 the Victoria Pioneer Rifle Company—'African Rifles'—was composed of fifty black volunteers under Captain Fortune Richard, the point being to protect the colony from American annexation (and the spectre of slavery). rusty arms, a self-built drill hall, uniforms designed and sewn by their wives. funded entirely by the black community. the sole militia in the colony. Douglas withheld funds. Fortune was denied his petition for arms and cash, while hundreds of rifles sat unused in Victoria's armory. eventually, the corps dissolved into a brass band.

3 Jacob Francis, lucky enough to have been born black in England, therefore a British subject, therefore allowed to run for office, lost a local election to a white opponent. when the opponent was disqualified for being absent at election time, Francis, ostensibly the winner, instead was disqualified by the Assembly on a technicality. his written petition was said to have too many `erasures and interlineations` in the body of the document.

HIDE AND GO SEEK

we play here behind the drill hall cause it's got plenty of bushes, but it's still close to home. we'll go through the rules one time for the new kid.

I   the drill hall back door is Home Free.

II   we do 'I Potato, II Potato' to see who's It.

III   we do 'Snakes, Snakes on Your Back' to see how much the It has to count. X seconds for each finger guessed wrong.

IV   the It has to count out loud, no whispering. and you have to count like this: 'I Mississippi, II Mississippi . . .'

V   when the It is done, he shouts, 'Ready or not, here I come!' really loud.

VI   if the It finds someone, he calls, 'I-II-III on' whoever it is, then runs like hell for Home Free. if the It beats the runner to Home Free, then the first runner caught will be the next It. he waits at Home Free until the It has found everybody.

VII   if the It doesn't catch the last runner—the last runner makes it to Home Free—that's called 'Save The Bunch.' everyone is saved and the It has to be It all over again.

VIII if the It finds someone and thinks it's someone else and the It calls out the wrong name, that's 'Rusty Nails.' everyone meets back at Home Free and the It has to start all over again.

IX   and remember: if you're It, you have to go out looking. you can't just hang around Home Free. absolutely no Home-Sucking.

okay, let's start. oh, I forgot to tell you: new kids are automatically It for their first game. now turn around so I can do 'Snakes, Snakes on Your Back, Which One is the One That Bit?'

EVENING AT THE COLONIAL

The Colonial Theatre, 1860. Victoria's first (segregated) playhouse.

+   one please. for the parquette.

-     I don't think so, darkie. not today. all I can sell you is balcony seating.

+   (aggressively dignified.) one ticket for the parquette, *sir* (spat out).

-     listen, we're not going through this with you people again: coloured seating . . .

+   'coloured seating,' he says.

-     . . . is in the balcony. If you don't like it, go back to the States. or go back to Africa while you're at it. but you ain't getting a seat down front *no* how.

+   'coloured seating,' he says. 'Africa,' he says.

-     are you causing trouble? do I have to get the constable?

+   'trouble,' he says.

-     you're pushing it, boy. keep pushing it.

+   'boy,' he says.

-     that's it, I'm calling the constable. you can sort this out among the two of you.

+   you've got no business sense, is what it is. you fools would
     open a sand shop in a desert if you thought you could make
     niggers stock the shelves. talkin bout, 'what I lose in sales I'll
     make back in labour costs.'

-    either buy a ticket for the balcony, or *exeunt*. let's go. I got real
     patrons waiting in line behind you.

+   (to a crowd, which has appeared like worms in unattended
     meat.) this, my fellow Victorians, is the rarest of the rare
     indeed. behold: a business based not on cash, but on ideas.
     watch this. (fans cash in the face of the wicket man.) not even a
     flinch or a lunge or a smacking of the chops. this is a business
     that has discovered the secret formula of industry, the fountain
     of youth, the lodestone of laissez-faire. (to the wicket man.)
     please decipher for me this miracle equation, this truth more
     elusive than Xanadu or the kingdom of Prestor John, this
     alchemy of mutable humanity: tell me how you run a business
     that requires not money from willing hands?

-    (looking puzzled.) are you trying to wind me up?

+   I wouldn't dream.

-    (looking resolved.) this wicket's closed to you, coon. go sharpen a
     spear.

+   and you? are you manufactured of glass? or marble? which? 'in
     his own image.' you don't believe a word of it, do you? you
     can't possibly have children. you can't possibly have a wife. you
     can't possibly . . .

     (but he loses heart. the face cannot see him, he knows it; none
     of them can, not even his own people. all he can think of is his
     daughter. there are blueberries flourishing behind the drill hall.
     he was talking to Fortune when she came out of the thicket

with Carver's boy. the two had the boy's ragged hat full of
berries. probably ruined a good hat. kids giggly. Fortune
ignored them, kept on about the Pig War. but he drifted while
Fortune talked, mesmerized, eyes on his daughter. she laughs
like there is no hurt, he thought. she pops the berries into her
mouth slowly and steadily like nothing runs out. then Carver's
boy pulled her braid. then she stuck her tongue out at him.
then her tongue was blue.)

BIOGRAPHY OF MIFFLIN WISTAR GIBBS

Philadelphia 1823

New York 1849

San Francisco 1850

Victoria 1858

Queen Charlotte Islands 1869

Oberlin 1870

Little Rock 1871

Tamatave 1898

Little Rock 1901

Kingdom Come 1915

EVENING AT THE COLONIAL

the word.

been a bit of a back and forth
in *The Colonist*. folks talkin bout,
'gonna be a riot down at The Colonial
if those niggers try to desegregate it.' truth told,

it's all these fucking Americans. I mean, what do you expect?
these British white folks are only mean on the inside. but Americans?
shit, home: watch your back round those sidewinders. truth be told,
if they take over, we're done for. better see you kissing that Union Jack,
Jack. when they play that 'Rule Britannia,' you best be dancing.
wanna see you put some ass in it, under
stand?

but you know that race man from Philly—Gibbs? *gots*
to like that guy. talk all proper and not anachronistic and shit.
heard he's gonna watch himself a show at The Colonial, say ain't
no man gonna stop him. all proper dicty brother. top hat and all that;
all that and then some. gotta like him.
our future lies in race men like that. they's us, and we's them. them blacks
'of letters,' as they say.

the scrap.

Gibbs and his party are somehow sold parquette tickets and take their seats
a few feet from the stage. before the curtains rise, one of the actors (an
Italian) refuses to sing until the blacks are deseated to the balcony. Gibbs,
his wife, his partner Pointer, and Pointer's daughter are attacked in their
seats, have a sack of flour thrown over them. Gibbs and Pointer fist back.
the actors leap off the stage to join the fray. the orchestra players grip their
horns like clubs, hot for the scrap. whites are fighting whites, Americans
sided up over the Civil War at home, and half the theatre is on the floor

beating on somebody. flour everywhere. stage lights cracked. seats pulled
out. someone gets it in the jaw with a trombone. the comedian grapples
with some ornery Yankee. constables come. pull people from people. Gibbs
gets a fistful of the fiddler's blond. papers and boos and ripped-up tickets
and fists and flour and nightsticks flying everywhere. someone falls into the
drum kit, elbow busting the snare's skin. Yankee on Rebel on Brit on cop
on black. Pointer's daughter hides behind the stand-up piano, covers her
head. a piece of the unperformed play's script floats down, lands on the
floor in front of her puzzled face.

the piece.

when she reads, her lips move.

> *older: north was the place to go. that idea is bred in the bone: north. a
> magical word. you go far enough north, you'll see the aurora borealis.
> do you know what that is?*
>
> *younger: colored lights in the sky. like a rainbow. a light show, but
> natural.*
>
> *older: well, sort of.*
>
> *younger: you ever seen it?*
>
> *older: have I ever seen it . . .*
>
> *younger: so what was it like?*
>
> *older: not like a rainbow, I'll tell ya. that's some stupid idea.*
>
> *younger: okay, not like a rainbow, but like what?*

older: different people say different things, but when I saw it, it was blue. I've heard tell of red and green and so forth. but when I saw it, it was blue.

younger: blue? just blue?

older: is there an echo in here? 'blue,' I said. know how a rainbow got seven colors—blue and six more? well, it's like that EXCEPT THERE AIN'T NO OTHER COLORS. just blue, blue, blue, blue, blue, blue, and blue.

Pointer's daughter laughs, folds the torn sheet, stashes it in her shoe.

WHERE HEAVEN LIES

1865 arrives
with January rain and Victoria mud,
departs
with the victory of North over
        South. the word in *The Mirror* is:

Emancipation at last!

sweet baby Jesus,
do you know what this means?
sweet baby Jesus, at last. at
last. praise be. after the cacophony
of war, we somehow sort of won. they saying we
emancipated
and pro
claimed. I read in *The Mirror* that they

're lining up to re
name themselves
down south. gonna have themselves a re
construction. gonna be some changes made.
even though the Captain caught a bullet through the centre
of his stovepipe hat in that theatre.

I can picture them,
all the brothers and the sisters,
down there
picking up the pieces,
though I'm missing from the frame. this dis

orientation is diz
zying. I can't play this game
no more; the croupier keeps changing

the rules. used to
believe the air was sweeter
on the Brit side of the border, freer
as of 1833, 49th degree, norther, nearer
to God and the top
of the world. Lord

been here seven years.
left everything.
renounced America.
what I got to show
for it? handful of magic
beens.

how anybody supposed to know
what crazy shit white folks are capable of?
who'da thought they'd do
something as out of character as setting us free?
headlines ought to read:

Hell freezes over; white people discover empathy

go figure.
got to be
something better
than this bullshit bitterness. a bet
ter prospect
maybe two steps
back,

cause Lord knows, in this pointless dis
persal, we ain't even one step forward here. our moment
nothing but a stutt

er
he
re.

PYRITES

six hundred of us streamed in in
the slip stream of slavery. landed at
Victoria, haven

where we was jumped in
to a gang called Brit in,
then Canada. in

tensionally, we shipped out out
west from the south,
and up north
from Frisc
o Bay. arriving,

soil alive under
Kwakiutl, Salish,
Songhee, and we,

and them, self
smuggling, taking, ex
tirpating every edge. sewing up
every angle. prying
gold from every fissure. sure
to interlineate every page
with 'amen' or 'shalt not.' faces white
as crosses. or flushed
with blood and un
uttered gunsmoke. cocking
the implications, in blue slapdash
Fort Victoria, Ararat, our own. us,

ready to call this what they want us to. to
put the 'it' in the British. not to make waves. to

strike it unpoor in the fields of gold, running over
with wheat and dandelions. sufferers
waiting on the age, more

than ore. integration
more than soil.
mining mining mining
wheat and dandelions, all the gold
a soul could hold. a here,
sweet enough to love enough
to never move. enough *enough*
to buy a loved one them
selves, and a ticket up.

April landing,
spring harvest.
Victoria pier,
Pyrrhic victory.

gettin lost
in the act of racing,
gettin got
in the act of chasing,
becoming behind
in the act of arriving. I

dance these Pyrrhic feet, these broken be
ats. this miner quay. homing in on a place called

From. folks dropped their to
ols in the fields to run. some
from as far as Mississippi, Carolina, Tennessee. re
moved out to California, up to some
British north of no
turning
back, like Lot. cast in a last

75

longing long shot. then,

seven years in, the ofays turn a
round and a
bolish the peculiar in
stitution. coast
clear. half of us here
in BC turn, head
for 'home,' hexed,
I'm convinced.
X and X
I and I
at the Trickster's behest
like a burr-headed country boy, be
wildered in the city's unbroken grey, getting taken
for a ride.

- I'll bet you a dollar I can tell you where you got your shoes, Mister.
+ a dollar? you gonna tell me where I got my shoes?

- that's right. you game?
+ okay, kid. so tell me where I got em then.

- you got em on the ground, nigger! ha, ha. now give me my dollar.
+ (nothing left to do but dig deep for change.)

THE BLUE ROAD: A FAIRY TALE

The wind bloweth where it listeth, and thou hearest the sound thereof, but canst not tell whence it cometh, and whither it goeth: so is every one that is born of the Spirit.

—John 3:8

The man had lived in the Great Swamp of Ink for as long as he could remember, and for as long as he could remember, he had always lived there alone. The swamp was made of the deepest and bluest ink in the world. The man's name was Lacuna.

One night, just before dawn, Lacuna tossed and turned unable to sleep. He sat up against a tree and wept. He was hungry and thirsty, but all there ever was to eat in the Great Swamp of Ink were bulrushes, and he was forced to drink the bitter-tasting ink to survive. He dreamed, as always, of leaving the terrible swamp. As he cried, he noticed the swamp brightening. Lacuna looked up to see a large glowing ball of light as bright as a sky full of full moons. He stood up rubbing the tears from his eyes, and stared at the ball of light that hovered above the blue marsh.

It spoke.

'My name is Polaris,' said the ball in a bottomless voice. 'I live in this swamp, but I have never seen you here before. What are you doing in my home?'

'I beg your pardon,' Lacuna replied, barely keeping his composure in the face of this very remarkable event. 'I don't mean to trespass. Are you a ghost?' He was terribly afraid of this talking ball of light.

'I am Polaris!' the ball shouted. 'I am a will-o'-the-wisp, the spirit of this bog. And I ask you again, what are you doing in my home?'

Lacuna was very frightened, but he was also very clever, and he saw an opportunity to escape the swamp.

'I'd gladly leave your home, Mr. Polaris, sir,' he said carefully, 'but I'm afraid I've lost my way. Since I can't remember which direction is home, I guess I'm just going to have to stay here.'

The will-o'-the-wisp grew larger and pulsated.

'You can't live here!' Polaris roared. 'This is *my* home. You must leave immediately or I will shine brighter and brighter and blind you with the light of a thousand suns!'

'Now look here, Mr. Polaris, there's no need to get angry.' Lacuna spoke soothingly. 'If you'll tell me the direction that I need to go to get home, and lead me to the edge of the swamp, I'll get out of here forever and let you be.'

'And you'll tell all the others like you to stay out of my home?' the will-o'-the-wisp persisted.

Lacuna, who was very clever, realized that other people may some day find themselves here in the Great Swamp of Ink. He thought very quickly of an answer that would not get them into trouble with the will-o'-the-wisp because he was not a selfish man, and he did not want others to be blinded.

'I'll be sure to tell people to stay clear of your swamp,' he said sincerely, 'but when I tell them about how big and shiny and pretty you are, I'm sure some of them will want to come and see you for themselves.'

Polaris' glow softened.

'Really?' he said wonderingly. 'You think they might come into the swamp just to see me?'

'Oh, of course they will! When I tell them how bright and sparkly you look, just like a star fallen loose from the sky, a few of the brave ones are bound to come just to catch a sight. They won't be wanting to stay, though—just to catch a sight and be on their way. I'm sure you can understand that?'

The will-o'-the-wisp was quiet for a moment, and Lacuna held his breath waiting for his answer.

'Well,' the will-o'-the-wisp said slowly, 'I can understand how some of your people might want to come and see me. I *am* rather dazzling, especially on clear nights like tonight. But if they come, they cannot stay! They can only catch a quick glimpse and then I will escort them immediately to the edge of the swamp! This is *my* home and no one else's. Surely you can understand the sanctity of one's home?'

Lacuna nodded gravely.

'And now it's time for you to leave. You have witnessed my beauty for long enough. Now tell me: which direction is your home?'

Lacuna had successfully tricked the will-o'-the-wisp into leading him out of the swamp, but now he was faced with a question that confused and confounded him more than any other: which way *was* his home? He didn't know. He visualized the four directions in his mind as if they were on a wheel, and in his mind he spun that wheel; the point was chosen.

'North.'

'North,' the spirit repeated. 'I'll take you to the northernmost margin of the Great Swamp of Ink.'

The will-o'-the-wisp picked up Lacuna and flew into the sky in a grand and luminous arc.

The Thicket of Tickets

Polaris gently set Lacuna down at the edge of the swamp, at the bottom of a steep grassy hill.

'Here is where we part,' the will-o'-the-wisp said. 'At the top of that hill you will find a vast briar called the Thicket of Tickets. If you can find your way through the thicket, they say there is a Blue Road that leads to the Northern Kingdom. There you will find others like yourself, and you will certainly live a better life than living in my swamp. Good luck.'

'Goodbye,' Lacuna said as he watched Polaris float back into the murk of the Great Swamp of Ink.

Lacuna climbed to the top of the hill and looked back in the direction he now knew was south: the vast swamp stretched out as far as he could see. He jumped up and clapped his hands together, then he did a little dance, because he realized that he was out of the inky wilderness forever. He looked at it and laughed out loud before turning northward, forever turning his back on the horrible swamp. He then noticed what faced him.

The Thicket of Tickets, as Polaris had called it, was the most dense briar he had ever seen. It stretched out to his left and right all the way beyond each horizon. There was no way to go but through it, or back into the swamp. He walked up to the thicket and examined its tangled mass.

The thicket consisted of coil upon coil of paper tickets, little squares of every colour, each with the words

Admit One

stamped on its surface in a stern black font. The coils were so tangled they reminded him of his hair when he did not comb it for several days; to pry it apart became a painful and daunting task. He reached his left arm in and found he could push the paper aside quite easily, however, so he stepped into the thicket with his entire body.

Lacuna soon found that he could walk through the Thicket of Tickets if he ripped the paper coils whenever he got too tangled. The only problem was that he could not see where he was going. He could not even see beyond his next footstep. He kept walking in faith but worried that at any moment he would step off a cliff, or into a tree or a rock. He stopped and pondered his situation after he had gone a dozen or so steps into the thicket.

'I can't go any farther,' he thought, 'because I don't know if I'm walking in a safe path or a dangerous one. I also can't be sure if I'm even heading north or not.' He thought and thought, because he was a clever man and he knew all sorts of tricks that had helped him survive worse situations than this.

Finally an answer came to him.

'I'll go back to the edge of the thicket and make a fire. Since this is only a paper briar, it will burn easily and quickly, and when all the tickets are burned up, I'll be able to see and walk all the way to the Blue Road and on to the Northern Kingdom!'

Lacuna started to walk back in the direction he had first come. After he had walked for what seemed like the same amount of time it took him to get this far into the thicket, he realized that he was not yet out. A wave of panic swept over him; he could not tell if he was actually walking in the same direction he had come because he could not see where he was going! He started to run, frantically ripping through the tickets, but by the time he ran out of breath, he was still nowhere near the edge. Or perhaps the edge was but a few steps away—he couldn't tell! For all his cleverness, the Thicket of Tickets had swallowed him up and he realized that he would just have to take a guess and walk in some random direction.

He walked for what seemed like days. He was hungry and thirsty and he even missed the horrible swamp because at least there were bulrushes and ink that he could eat and drink. He walked and walked, and his legs were painfully tired, but he knew he had no choice but to continue. Lacuna lost all track of time; he didn't know whether it was day or night. He could only hope that he was heading north, and in his desperate state he began to wonder if north was even the best way to go anyway. Lacuna began to miss the old swamp desperately, and cursed himself for leaving it in the first place.

'Surely I could have tricked Polaris into letting me stay,' he thought. Lacuna wanted to cry, but he was so thirsty and dry no tears would come, which made him even sadder. His feet and legs ached. The edges of the tickets cut his skin in a thousand tiny slices. He was tortured.

Just when he had resigned himself to the idea that he would soon die, but at least he would die walking until he collapsed of exhaustion, the coils of tickets got thinner and thinner until suddenly he found himself in the open air.

He emerged from the thicket at the top of a grassy hill. It was sunny and bright, and his vision was blurry from spending so long in darkness, and he tried wearily to focus. At the bottom of the hill he could make out what looked like trees. Weakened and half-blinded by the full light of day, Lacuna started down the hill. His aching legs gave out, and he fell, tumbling down the slope in a jumble of arms and legs and bruises.

When he finally stopped rolling, Lacuna felt his cheek was resting on the cold, hard ground. He realized it was not grass, but stone. He sat up slowly and stiffly and found himself on a dark blue cobblestone road that ran from the bottom of the hill off into a dense forest. The faint sound of running water could be heard from beyond the trees, and he knew he had come out on the far side of the terrible thicket. Perhaps there would be fish in that stream, he thought.

The bricks of the road were a beautiful sight, bright and rich, though they were startlingly close to the colour of the ink in the Great Swamp of Ink. Although Lacuna was very happy to have found this Blue Road to the Northern Kingdom, he couldn't help but wish it were a different colour.

After a day of resting and regaining his strength, he turned his thoughts to the Thicket of Tickets.

'If people find themselves trying to cross the thicket like me, they won't realize how easy it is to get lost in there. I was lucky to survive, let alone make it to the right destination. I had a good idea to burn it, but I thought it too late.' Because he was not a selfish man, but one who often thought of others, he decided to go back and set fire to the dangerous thicket.

Lacuna took a burning stick from his campfire and proceeded up the hill.

He cast the stick into the tangled mass of tickets. As he had suspected, the paper caught fire instantly and burned fiercely. He had to retreat down the hill to avoid the intense heat of the fire. From the edge of the forest he watched the whole Thicket of Tickets burn to a pile of ashes. For a moment he felt a strange sadness seeing such a curious thicket destroyed by his own hand, but he knew it was for the best.

'Now,' he thought, 'no one will face the troubles I had to face if they make it this far.'

Satisfied, he set out on the Blue Road.

The way through the forest was long but pleasant. The road was well-kept and food was more plentiful and infinitely more nourishing here than in the Great Swamp of Ink. On his journey, he picked fruit from wild trees, fished in streams, and gathered dark berries. Lacuna was still lonely, but he consoled himself with the knowledge that the Northern Kingdom was at the end of this road, and even if it were far, the travelling was easy. He sang songs to himself as he walked, to make himself feel less lonely; he sang songs about his loneliness. He dreamed of a place where he could settle down. He tried to imagine what the Northern Kingdom would be like, but the thought of it frightened him a little. Lacuna was very clever, and he knew that kingdoms were not always good. 'The Northern Kingdom' *sounded* wonderful; the words felt good on his tongue. But what did he really know of this place he was seeking?

Up to now, Lacuna had drunk water straight out of the stream, but he decided to fill his canteen so he could sip the river water while he walked. When he pulled the canteen from his back pocket and opened it, he realized it was full of the ink that he used to drink when he had lived in the swamp. He smiled, thinking about how he would never have to drink ink again, but he decided he would keep the canteen full of it as a souvenir and a reminder of where he had come from. This way, he would never forget his past.

Finding the canteen full of ink caused Lacuna's thoughts to drift to the swamp. He thought about Polaris and how he had tricked that old will-o'-the-wisp. Although he had flattered Polaris to trick him, he now realized for the first time that Polaris really was pretty. His brightness *was* dazzling and beautiful, but somehow, in the telling of his trick, Lacuna had not even realized the truth of this.

As he walked and thought, Lacuna noticed a small booth beside the road up ahead in the distance. When he got closer to it, he also noticed a strip of seven colours painted across the Blue Road; it looked like a rainbow cutting across his path. An old man in a blue suit and a blue hat sat next to the booth on a wobbly two-legged stool. This old-timer himself only had one leg. A strange-looking crutch leaned against the wall of the booth, next to him.

'Hello,' said Lacuna to the old man. 'I'm on my way to the Northern Kingdom. Are you from there?'

'Am I *from* there?' the old man snapped in an angry voice. 'No, I'm not *from* there. You don't know much, do you?' He stared at Lacuna without a trace of humour in his eyes.

Lacuna felt annoyed at this unprovoked attack. He quickly decided that since this old man was not from the Northern Kingdom, and was not very friendly, he would just be on his way.

'I have to be going,' he said curtly, and he started down the Blue Road once more.

'Hey, wait a minute, wait a minute!' the old man shouted frantically, jumping up out of his seat, which promptly fell over. Lacuna stopped still, startled by the man's sudden outburst. The old-timer limped onto the road with the aid of his strange-looking crutch.

'Don't you see what's right in front of your eyes, boy?' He was pointing at the rainbow painted across the Blue Road.

'Yeah, so?' Lacuna said. He wanted to get going.

'That's the *border*. You can't just up and cross the border like that. What's the matter, have you lost your mind?'

'So what am I supposed to do?' Lacuna said impatiently. He began to wonder if this old man was insane. He wanted to be on his way northward.

'Listen to me, boy, because obviously there's a whole lot you don't know about this world. *That* is the *border*,' he said, pointing again at the rainbow painted on the road, 'and I'm the Border *Guard*. You can't cross the border until *I* say so.' He shifted his weight from his good leg to his crutch. Lacuna, now that he was up close to the Border Guard, could see that his crutch was actually a huge skeleton key.

'There are rules involved,' the Border Guard added cryptically. 'I'll need your ticket,' he said, holding out his hand.

Lacuna immediately remembered the Thicket of Tickets he had burned to the ground. He felt a sinking feeling in the pit of his stomach.

'I don't have a ticket,' he said quietly.

'You don't have a ticket?' the Border Guard snapped. 'Then you can't pass. That's the rules: no ticket, no road.'

'But I have to go to the Northern Kingdom,' Lacuna said, trying to keep the sound of desperation out of his voice. 'How am I supposed to get there if I don't keep following the road?' He was angry and frustrated, and wondered if he should even listen to this strange Border Guard with his crazy skeleton key crutch. After all, how did he know that the Border Guard had any real authority over the Blue Road? Polaris hadn't told him anything about this. But then again perhaps Polaris didn't know about the border. Lacuna considered crossing it without the Border Guard's permission; he was only an old man with one leg, and he wouldn't be able to stop a young man like himself. However, perhaps the Border Guard worked for the Northern Kingdom, and not following these rules would get him into trouble when he finally got there.

'Isn't there some way of continuing on the Blue Road, Mr. Border Guard?' he asked politely. 'I really desperately need to go to the Northern Kingdom. I have nowhere else to go.'

'Well,' the Border Guard said slowly, 'according to the rules, there *is* a way for people who don't have a ticket. But it isn't easy.' He grinned enigmatically. 'Have you ever seen a dance called "the limbo"? Two people hold a stick a few feet off the ground and the dancer leans way back and shuffles underneath the stick.'

Lacuna nodded. He knew the dance.

'Well, if you can limbo under the border, you may pass freely. That's all I can do for you.'

Lacuna looked at the border again: it was painted onto the road. There was no way anyone could limbo beneath a painted border.

'Oh, and you can't dig underneath it,' the Border Guard added, 'you have to dance under it, you have to limbo underneath the border. It's nothing personal, son. I'm just following the rules.'

Lacuna could barely contain his anger, but he knew he needed to remain calm and think of some way out of this situation. He carefully considered his circumstances. He knew that no one can limbo beneath a painted border. He thought and thought but could see no way out of his predicament.

There was nothing else to do but set up a camp beside the Border Guard's booth and wait until an idea came to him.

How the Man Limbo Danced Beneath a Painted Border

For four days, Lacuna camped beside the Border Guard's booth. During these days he passed the time by playing cards with the Border Guard. Once while they were playing cards he noticed a tiny starling flying low to the ground; it was heading north towards the border. Just as the little bird was about to cross the place where the border was, the Border Guard lept from his two-legged stool (which promptly fell over), hopped on his good leg towards the bird, and chopped the bird in half in mid-flight with the edge of his skeleton key crutch. He did this all in one dazzlingly swift motion, whereupon he returned to his two-legged stool to continue their card game. Lacuna was dumbfounded at the unlikely speed and agility that the Border Guard showed, not to mention the horror of seeing the tiny bird sliced in half.

'Sorry about the interruption,' the Border Guard said, 'but no one can cross the border without properly observing the rules.'

'Not even birds?' Lacuna asked incredulously.

'Nobody at all,' the Border Guard answered firmly. He went on to explain that his skeleton key crutch also doubled as an axe. In fact, according the Border Guard, it was the sharpest axe in the world, capable of slicing easily through any material. Lacuna realized that now more than ever he had to think of a way to limbo beneath the painted border.

On the fourth night of camping, while he tossed and turned unable to sleep, he finally came up with a plan.

When he awoke in the morning, Lacuna stretched for awhile, then stood pondering the sky. He carefully studied the clouds and the horizon. He then breakfasted with the Border Guard.

That afternoon while they were playing cards over lunch, Lacuna periodically looked up and observed the sky. When night fell he bedded down and slept soundly until the morning.

This pattern continued for three more days. On the third day after Lacuna had had his idea, the Border Guard finally asked him what he was going to do. It had been raining all morning, and the two of them sat at the table inside the booth playing their afternoon game of cheat. The sun was just beginning to emerge from behind the coal-coloured clouds.

'So what are you going to do, boy?' the Border Guard asked him. 'You can't stay camped here forever, although I suppose there's no rule against it. I don't mind the company but I just don't think you're ever going to be able to limbo underneath that painted border. It just can't be done.'

While he talked, Lacuna was staring out the window and into the sky.

'Are you a betting man, Mr. Border Guard?'

The Border Guard eyed him cautiously.

'Well, that depends on what the bet is, doesn't it?'

'Yes, it does,' Lacuna said seriously. He thought about how he had burnt the Thicket of Tickets to help the people that might follow him, without knowing that they would need those tickets to get across this border. Now he would make up for his mistake.

'I'll bet you your skeleton key crutch that I'll limbo beneath the border today. If I don't succeed, I'll give you all of what little money I have.'

The Border Guard shook his head.

'That's a stupid bet to make, boy. It can't be done. I'd be taking your money, as sure as you're born.'

Lacuna held his gaze steadily. 'Will you bet me or not?'

The Border Guard scratched his head and wondered at the younger man's stupidity.

'Why not? If you want to give your money away, I'll take it. Sure. Why not? But if you walk down that road without limbo dancing beneath the border like I said, I'll have to cut you in half just like I did that bird. I hope you understand that.'

Lacuna nodded.

'I'm going to go pack up my campsite. When I'm finished, you'll watch me limbo beneath the border.'

The Border Guard shook his head in disbelief as Lacuna left the booth to pack up his gear.

While he was outside of the booth, Lacuna examined the sky once more. Satisfied, he went to his campsite and rummaged around in his knapsack until he found the canteen filled with ink from the Great Swamp of Ink. He then went to the Blue Road and poured the ink over the painted rainbow border. Since the ink was the exact colour of the Blue Road, the painted border was completely blotted out. He finished packing up his things and returned to the Border Guard's booth.

'Well, I'm ready to limbo beneath the border. And remember: if I succeed you have to give me your skeleton key crutch.'

'And *when* you fail, you'll have to give me all your money. And I'll most likely have to chop you in half.'

The two of them went to the spot on the Blue Road where the border had been, but the border was nowhere to be seen. The Border Guard was panic-striken.

'But where is it?' he shouted. 'The border's gone!'

Lacuna smiled and pointed into the sky.

Both men looked up to see an arcing rainbow far above them among the shifting clouds and sunlight.

'There it is,' Lacuna said sharply.

The Border Guard stared silently at the rainbow, completely baffled by this unthinkable turn of events. He looked back at Lacuna, utterly perplexed, but could not think of a single thing to say.

Lacuna slung his pack over his shoulder, bent backwards ever-so-slightly, and limbo danced a few steps down the Blue Road, beneath the rainbow that hung fast in the sky above them. He then turned around and held out his hand toward the Border Guard.

'I did it. Now give me your skeleton key crutch.'

The Border Guard's mouth hung open. He still could say nothing, but he looked at his crutch. Without it he would no longer be able to properly guard the border.

'Give me the crutch,' Lacuna persisted. He thought for a moment about something the Border Guard had said to him. 'Listen: we made a deal. I'm just following the rules.'

The Border Guard reluctantly handed him the skeleton key crutch, which Lacuna snatched out of his hand. He immediately turned his back on the Border Guard, laughed, and headed down the Blue Road, and on towards the Northern Kingdom.

If he had turned around to look, which he didn't, he would have seen the Border Guard balancing on his one leg, his mouth still open in disbelief. The Border Guard stared down at the road, then up at the rainbow, then down at the road again. He continued to do this until long after Lacuna had dropped out of sight in the distance.

The Gates of the Northern Kingdom

Once past the border, Lacuna's journey was easy. He reflected upon his incident with the Border Guard and felt confident he had done the right thing. He used the skeleton key crutch-axe as a walking stick, and he cheerfully sang to himself as he walked the Blue Road.

After several days of uneventful travel, Lacuna at last saw a great city looming on the horizon. As he got closer he could see that the Blue Road led straight to its gates, through a high alabaster-coloured wall that surrounded the city. Lacuna knew from its magnificence that this had to be the Northern Kingdom itself.

As he approached the gates, Lacuna passed several people, some coming in or out of the city, others selling goods by the side of the road. He marvelled that the people looked just like he did, but were all shapes, sizes, and ages. He was overwhelmed at seeing so many people in one place after seeing so few for so long—and this was only the outskirts of town. His mind boggled when he thought about how many more people there would be inside the vast metropolis.

He noticed several Gate Keepers checking people's bags and letting them through the massive portcullis. When it was Lacuna's turn to enter the city, a Gate Keeper stopped him.

'Your papers,' the Gate Keeper said tersely.

Lacuna wasn't sure what to do. He remembered the Border Guard; perhaps he was supposed to have gotten papers from the Border Guard that would allow him passage into the Kingdom.

'I don't have any papers, sir,' he said to the Gate Keeper. 'I'm not from here. I come from the, uh, south.' He had begun to say that he was from the Great Swamp of Ink, but decided that it might not make a very good impression; he wanted to erase his past forever and start again as a northern person, so he decided right there that he would mention the swamp as little as possible from now on.

'Go over there,' the Gate Keeper said, pointing to a small stone gatehouse. He proceeded to inspect the next person's papers.

Lacuna approached the gatehouse and knocked on the door. Another Gate Keeper opened it and let him in.

'What can I do for you?'

'Well, sir, the man at the gate asked me for my papers and I told him I don't have any papers. See, I'm not from here, I'm from the south. Was I supposed to get my papers at the border?'

'The border?' the Gate Keeper said with a frown. 'I don't know what you're talking about. He was asking you for your papers of citizenship. You have to have papers to prove that you are a citizen of the Northern Kingdom to enter, of course.'

Lacuna felt despair welling in his chest. He had come so far, only to be denied.

'What am I going to do?' he asked desperately.

'Don't worry,' the Gate Keeper said, beginning to grasp Lacuna's situation. He shook his head and moved his hand as if to wave away Lacuna's worries like so much smoke.

'Have a seat. Listen, I have the authority to issue you papers immediately. All you have to do is register here, and sign some forms.'

The Gate Keeper pushed a stack of papers towards Lacuna.

'It's just so we know who you are. If you sign the papers and become a citizen, you can come and go as you please. You can leave the Kingdom and return any time you want. We welcome new subjects. All you have to do is fill out the forms and sign on the dotted line, and you'll be an instant citizen.'

He passed a quill pen and a small pot of blue ink across his desk to where Lacuna sat listening intently.

'There's only one rule that I have to inform you of before you sign.'

As he spoke, the Gate Keeper's eyes strayed absent-mindedly to the wall of his office. Lacuna followed the man's gaze to a portrait that hung there depicting a stern-looking man wearing a crown full of enormous sapphires. The Gate Keeper cleared his throat and continued without taking his eyes off the portrait.

'Citizens like yourself are required to take possession of a special mirror, which they are to carry on their person at all times. Now listen carefully: *as long as you are within the gates of the city you must never take your eyes off this mirror.* The mirror is magical, and if you look away from it for even a second, you will feel a sharp pain that will grow in intensity until it eventually kills you; all this will only take a matter of minutes. However, if you close your eyes entirely, you will not feel any pain. But as long as your eyes are open, you must be gazing into the mirror. That way, you may sleep at night quite normally, provided you do not open your eyes until the mirror is in front of you when you wake up.'

Lacuna could not believe what he was hearing. A magical mirror from which he wasn't allowed to break his gaze?

'This is insane,' he protested. 'How will I get around? How will I hold a job or even walk down the street if I always have to look into this magical mirror? Does everyone in the Northern Kingdom have to do this?'

The Gate Keeper sighed as if he had explained this far too many times to feel altogether sympathetic.

'Only people who were not born in the city are assigned mirrors. Those who were born here do not need them. As for getting around, I assure you that the Mirror People—as we call citizens like yourself—do just fine. They manage to hold down jobs and raise families, and they get around the best they can. Believe me, it may seem strange now but you'll adjust in no time. And if you can't, well, you can always go back where you came from.'

Lacuna felt a horrid mixture of disappointment, anger, and frustration. He wished he had gone west or east or south: anywhere but here. But he had come so far that he was determined at least to see this great city with all its people. He reached for the papers, dipped the quill pen in the pot of deep blue ink, and signed on the dotted line. Immediately afterward, the Gate Keeper brought forth a large golden-framed mirror from beneath his desk and handed it to him. It was heavy and unwieldy, as wide as Lacuna's shoulders, and square. He took it grudgingly and returned to the gates with his freshly-validated papers.

Once inside the city, the first thing Lacuna noticed was that he had to strap everything onto his back, including his skeleton key crutch-axe, because it took both of his hands to hold the magical mirror in front of his face. He also noticed that the Gate Keeper was not lying about the intense pain that came to him when he glanced away for merely a moment to take in the city; the pain shot like lightning through his temples, and out of necessity he quickly returned his gaze to the mirror. He noticed, however, that there were several people on the streets that held mirrors up to their faces, although the majority of the people in the city did not. He saw that the Mirror People walked backwards using their mirrors to see over their shoulders which direction they were going. It looked like many of these people had been doing this for years because they seemed very skilled at walking backwards, talking to each other, and even reading words in books or newspapers backwards, all by angling the mirror in the right direction. They looked awkward, but managed as best they could.

He spent his first day walking around the city, trying to get used to walking backwards and with his mirror as his guide, looking for a place to stay and places that might hire him for work. He felt foolish with his mirror, especially when he was around people who did not need mirrors.

At one point, he had to ask directions of a man who also carried a mirror, and for the first time realized that such a conversation meant that they both had to stand back to back each holding his mirror so as to see over his shoulder into the other person's mirror. He did not actually get to look directly into the man's face but rather he was seeing a reflection of a reflection of the man talking to him.

After several days of orienting himself, Lacuna started working, shining mirrors on a street corner for pocket change. He polished mirrors for the Mirror People who were busily going to and fro in the great city. He also found a cheap rooming house that he could afford, and spent his days working hard and wondering what his future would bring.

'I'm happy to be here,' he thought to himself as he shined an old woman's mirror, 'and I know this is better than the Great Swamp of Ink, but it isn't what I expected at all.' His thoughts circled around in his mind like seagulls over a low tide, but they would not perch at a conclusion. He was not happy, nor was he entirely sad; he was puzzled.

'You're awfully quiet there, young man.'

The old woman's voice caught Lacuna's attention. He looked up at her: she was a dignified-looking woman, and she sat in the little chair he had set up for customers, her eyes closed as he was busy polishing her mirror.

'I was just thinking about the Kingdom,' he said to the woman. 'I'm still trying to get used to these mirrors, to tell you the truth, ma'am.'

'Don't you worry about it, youngster,' she said kindly. He could hear in her voice that she cared and understood how he felt. 'It might take a while, but you'll get the hang of it. Soon you'll barely notice that you have that mirror. It becomes like a friend after awhile.'

'I still don't understand why we have to have them at all,' he said.

'Now, that kind of talk is foolishness,' the old woman retorted. 'It's just the way things are. The King wants it that way, and this is the Northern Kingdom, right? There's no point in not understanding something as simple as that.'

When he finished polishing her mirror, Lacuna put it into her hands. She opened her eyes and examined how well he had cleaned the glass and, satisfied, reached into her purse to pay him. Her eyes, in the angle of her mirror, fixed on the skeleton key crutch-axe which lay at Lacuna's side. He had gotten into the habit of carrying it around with him wherever he went.

'What's that?' she asked.

'It's a crutch. And an axe, sort of.' He realized that he wasn't very sure what to call it. 'It's mine,' he offered finally.

'It's pretty,' said the old woman. 'I've never seen anything like it. It's unusual. I bet you could make an interesting costume for the Festival around something that unusual.'

'What festival?' Lacuna asked.

'What do you mean, "What festival?" *The* Festival. Only the biggest event of the year. You really must not be from around here. Once a year we have a celebration called the Festival of the Aurora Borealis. The great Aurora Borealis comes out and lights up the whole sky above the Kingdom. It's an unbelievably dazzling light show, and everyone wears strange and unique costumes for the occasion. We all look up into the sky and at midnight the

Aurora Borealis arrives in all its glory. The Festival is only a month and a half away. You watch, business will pick up around the time before the Festival. Everyone will be getting their mirrors polished so they can see the lights best.'

With that, the woman paid Lacuna, thanked him, and went on her way.

For the next few nights, he found it difficult to sleep. Thoughts circled in his head like his hand circled with its cloth when he polished someone's mirror. He realized that since he had come to the Northern Kingdom he had barely spoken to a Mirrorless Person, and the only Mirror People he knew were those he met as he worked. Amazingly, he still felt lonely even though he was surrounded by people. He hated carrying his mirror around all day, and it took all his patience to keep from smashing it every time he thought about how foolish it all seemed. He wondered if he would go on forever at this job, living in a tiny room, and feeling alone. But the Festival of the Aurora Borealis was something to look forward to. Surely the Aurora Borealis would be at least as beautiful as Polaris. Lacuna wondered if he should really make a costume using the skeleton key crutch-axe as the old woman had suggested. Perhaps he would dress up as the Border Guard. He thought that it would be such a pity that he and all the Mirror People would have to watch the Aurora Borealis through these stupid mirrors. He had had the experience of witnessing Polaris up close with his own eyes, and he didn't realize what a privilege that had been until this moment.

With these disjointed thoughts spinning in his head, Lacuna drifted off to sleep.

The Festivals of the Aurora Borealis

He woke abruptly out of a startling dream, and immediately opened his eyes by reflex; instantly, the pain rushed in. He groped for his mirror, which lay beside the bed and looked into it. By the time the mirror was safely in front of his eyes, he realized that he had already forgotten his dream.

Later in the day, while polishing an accountant's mirror, Lacuna suddenly remembered what his dream had been about.

He had dreamt of a vast sheet of ice. Lacuna wore a pair of skates and glided effortlessly across the ice. He felt as if he were flying; he felt just as he did when Polaris carried him through the air out of the Great Swamp of Ink. Lacuna skated in large figure-eights, looping a broad curve, then arcing back across his previous path. His skates cut a massive figure into the ice that looked like this:

$$\infty$$

He skated and skated around and around on the ice. That was all.

When he remembered this dream, Lacuna stopped still in his polishing. An idea had finally come to him.

With his mirror, he looked up at the accountant sitting in the customer's chair; the accountant wore a pair of wire-rimmed glasses. Lacuna quickly checked his pockets to see how much money he had on him. He handed the accountant back his mirror, so that they could see each other.

'Listen, sir,' Lacuna said, 'can I buy those glasses from you? I'll give you this.' He held out a week's earnings to the accountant.

The accountant frowned and looked at the money, then back at Lacuna.

'That's a lot of money. Why would you want to buy my glasses? If your eyesight is bothering you, you ought to go to the optometrist. You need to get glasses that work for you specifically. They're unique that way, you know.'

Lacuna shook his head and thrust the money at the accountant.

'No, no, I don't need them for that. Please take my money, it's more than enough to buy a new pair. I just need your glasses right now.'

'Are you feeling all right?' the accountant asked suspiciously. None of this made sense to him, and, after all, he had only wanted his mirror shined.

Lacuna was getting impatient and blurted out, 'Look, I'm fine, I'm fine. Will you please sell me your glasses right away? Please? I mean, if you don't want the money, I'll find someone else.'

The accountant was reluctant, but he knew that the money was enough to buy a newer and better pair, and he really didn't care much if a crazy mirror polisher wanted to throw his money away on foolish things. He took the money, and gave Lacuna his glasses, but waited around to see what this crazy mirror polisher was going to do with them.

Lacuna took the accountant's glasses and immediately smashed the lenses out of them. The accountant shook his head, certain now that the poor boy had lost his mind. But then Lacuna carefully picked all the glass out of the frames of the spectacles until there was nothing but the wire rims. He lay his own mirror on the ground and picked up the skeleton key crutch-axe, which was at his side as always. He paused for a moment, remembering that the Border Guard had said the skeleton key crutch-axe was the sharpest blade in the whole world. He carefully pressed the blade of the axe against the glass of his mirror and cut out a small circle. The blade sliced easily through the glass, as easily as if he were dipping it into water. He gently lifted up the small circle of mirror and fitted it into one of the frames of the wire rims. The accountant watched speechlessly, and a small crowd began to gather. Lacuna put the small circle of mirror into the frame so that the piece of mirror faced inward. Then he put on the glasses. His left eye stared directly into the piece of mirror, while his right eye scanned the crowd, the buildings, and the sky directly; there was no pain because he had not broken eye contact with the piece of mirror with one eye, while his other eye was free to see the world plain.

The crowd grew until the whole corner was buzzing with people. The ones who had been there to witness the event were telling the newcomers, and people were talking to one another excitedly. Everyone was visibly awed, and some actually gasped when they heard the news that this young mirror polisher had figured out a way to see with one eye on and one eye off his cursed mirror.

The accountant, who had watched the whole spectacle, said, 'Boy, will you make me a pair of glasses like that? I'll give you double your money back.'

Suddenly, everyone pushed forward, some waving money at Lacuna, dozens of Mirror People asking him to make them a pair of the miraculous glasses. Right there on the street, he set about to making dozens of pairs of glasses for those who had the money and the frames. In less than an hour, he had made more money than he had ever dreamed of. The accountant offered Lacuna his financial services, which he accepted because he was too busy making glasses to handle the great crowd. The accountant organized the excited Mirror People into a line-up. By the end of the day, Lacuna had made enough money to live in leisure for years.

In the next few weeks, Lacuna opened up a shop and hired the accountant as his personal assistant. He used his idea and his skeleton key crutch-axe-glasscutter to accumulate for himself a small fortune. In the days leading up to the Festival of the Aurora Borealis, business, as the old woman had predicted, boomed. Everyone wanted the new glasses; everyone wanted to see the world directly with at least one eye, and without the medium of their cursed mirror. In time, he knew, other people would take his idea and start their own businesses with ordinary glasscutters, but he had already firmly established himself.

On the eve of the Festival of the Aurora Borealis, Lacuna and the accountant dressed up for the event, the accountant in a dazzling rented costume of silver and gold, Lacuna in a tailored blue approximation of the Border Guard's uniform. The two partners strutted out into the night to join the greatest celebration of the year in the Northern Kingdom. As they walked through the crowd, Lacuna thought about how fortunate he had been. Many of the Mirror People walked around in the glasses that he had made for them, excited to see their first Festival inside the city with one good eye. It was true that there were Mirror People who still held the old, large mirrors—those who couldn't afford to buy his new innovation—but he generally avoided looking at them. There were also the ones outside the walls of the city. He had learned that it was a tradition for many Mirror People to leave the city on this night to watch the Aurora Borealis from the countryside where they didn't need their cursed mirrors. There, some Mirror People had always gathered together to create their own Festival. He wondered about them, and he wondered about the ones who still held their large, cumbersome mirrors. He even wondered what the Mirrorless People thought about all the recent changes he had sparked. He wondered about these things, but his thoughts just circled in his head, round and round like the alabaster walls of the city.

At midnight, the Aurora Borealis arrived. It was beautiful, and everyone in the crowd gasped and cheered at its wavering colours. The lights danced and weaved across the sky, and everyone, in their brilliant and bizarre costumes, began the traditional dances that imitated the vacillations and the shimmer of the Aurora Borealis itself.

Lacuna stood still, among his people, looking up, gaping at the motion of the lights with one half of his vision, staring at his own open eye with the other.

THE COVER

I can make a ship sail on dry land.

—The Temptations

fifties

LEGBA, LANDED

he crossed. the border
line in a northern corner

       four
cardinal   points
     for

a better over there. created a here.

one foot in A   one foot in a
merica.   Canada.

          one Negro,
           liminal.
           limped
            a

cross
clutching a crutch
       a sliver of a quest
       a lining of silver
       a sparkle of meridian
       a severed scent
       a razorous rain
       a glade
       a terrain
       a blame

a strait razorous border. he
reached for a me
to be
real

real
real
enough to re
treat into a tree
for the forests he could see
he sought as he believed himself
into the mirrorous glass a
cross the border.

customs: are you carrying any
baggage? are you moving any fruit or seeds or trees
of knowledge, immortality or weeds or roots or truths
through to bluer blues and greener
grass, hash, heroin, hidden, stashed
uppers, Canada, land. no lower-class
middle passage. no flask
of flashing yellow magma,
spirits, rum, release. no fire
arms, tobacco, or too much cash.
or too little cash.
in the razor-thin space between my lines,
you may fit in. line up
and pay your sin
tax
at
the next
wicket.

here eyes bear the white burden
of watchful wardens
dutiful citizens in
lower mainlands
patrol each shade of un
white. each stray curl of un
straight. each singular hint of un
settled seeking for   home

carry me, motherless child.
my tracks are so sweet to the stalker.
Mount Zion, baptize me abysmal.
Abyssinian of obsidian meridians.
I take to the night like winged carrion.
I am sweet to the stalker.
like an ibis, stems snapped
like reeds, I fly above
reptiles and annihil
ation. forever in flight against the sky.
painted feathers brushing versus eternity.
limbs in the image dangle.
snapped like photos.
finished like the tape breaks up
lifting the race. winged
in flight
without hope
of landing. Canada
geese band together
to kill their crippled
for fear of attracting
stalkers to the flock.
they peck.
a mess of splintered feathers.
hollowed bones.
shattered limbs.
frenzy toward the nest of night.
death.
no.
rest.
I am sweet to the prey.
my only thought: I fly on,
on, my sky home,
home

THE BOOK

woke up this mornin, had to be long
gone. cided it was time to get to
steppin. woke up this mornin,

felt fulla holes. gaps. my pupils di
lated so wide, I

disappeared. think it's time
to turn this silver in my pocket in
to a ticket. take the sacred
parallel lines and aim my

self like a breeze. to leave
is as easy as breathing. to leave
is as easy as steam steaming. to leave
the god forsaken south. northbound. gold

veins the only blood running
under
the border
coming up whole in a whole new belonging
gone. the sweet bye and good

Lord, take my hand. precious
Lord, take this hand and point it. Lord,
I know you can keep a straight
face. ain't no place

to be, here. sound
of the stones going, 'Canaan land.'
fulla honey. going, 'steal way.' stage
whispering. breeze blowing. knowing only
one way, one direction. flowing. crossing.

Jordan. done. time. to tell you. how
I got over. forty-nine

dollars to my name. in my sole. at the line,
finally. like a wave
on a beach. as they say,
'floodgates.' gettin eyed. ID'ed. gettin ?'ed.
gettin searched. I keep up my
passport-photo-wide smile. I's artfully averted. comes

the question: 'any drugs?'
thinking: 'you offering?' going: 'nope.'
the questioner: 'you say dope?'
'nope.'
eyeing: 'sit while I check your bag.'
finding the Bible.
flipping, slowly, page to page.
I: 'this is gonna take forever.'
eye: 'might be drugs hidden between the pages.
just sit there till I make sure you're clean.'
he flips the pages
slowly. an all-day-taking pace. others stream
past. name
on his tag says Peter O'Something. heard it said
the Irish are niggers turned inside out. he flips

the pages slowly. disinterestedly. playing with me.
there's nothing. cuts deeper. than time.

question: 'you a pimp?'
self: 'hell, no.'
O'Something: 'did you just curse? did I hear you correctly?'
I: 'how'm I supposed to know what you can and can't hear?'

stare.

'you won't be coming into my country today.'
shutting.

'next time watch your mouth.'
next.

AU

but tomorrow is another day. changing

of the god. sliding
in on a moonbeam. may
as well be. and finally

on the town, with no bank.
on the town, with no hustle.
on the town, with no. but dig it: I'm no

rth, and that's damn
near nough. poured
my whole fold in
to my threads. drop dead
fines. conked head. on time.
say so myself, hand

some
where. shining
like my last dime. new in town. on it.
and the future's the future.
and I look it in the eye.
empty and mine.

THROUGH

ghosts populate your shoulder
if you ain't careful. work up through you
like a dandelion in a side
walk crack. like a little aged afro, colour
of come. accent

fading. deferring. smoking
reefer on Keefer Street with Fuller,
Drew, and Half Chinese Marie. singin
songs from Motor City. (all roads lead
to Berry Gordy.) walkin in a winter hinter
land. so high,

we can't even get down. brim riding so low,
chin up just to see. so in. and only
ghosts hate new things, but dig anachronisms. walk
through walls chasing em. on Main there's a joint
keeps the box fulla long plays. one side for a dime. damn,
can't be a drum cause you can't beat that.

THE BRIDGE

call this what? place ghost-
ridden. hell,
I should be happy: a hotel
room, blue venues, good enough jukes,
cool clubs, pool rooms, parlours, and the truth
in the person of Jesus Christ in pinstripes
droppin his last two bits on a camel's hair coat. out

to do the dip with Half Chinese Marie. hummin
'Work With Me Annie' despite us all.

so work with me.

blessed are the drummers for they are in four four.
blessed are the mothers above the numbers.
blessed are the lovers fuckin with the fighters.
blessed are the good tippers.
blessed are the others.
blessed are the ones who'll stay.

say in

take it to the bridge. watch me. I got it.
by the toe.

FACING THE BLUES

three face
down. on a corner in the closest thing
we got to dark
town.

keep your eye
on the black lady. you
look like smart money. I
see that you're the kind
that knows what's what. now,
what's what?

nice try. maybe next
time. keep your eye
on the black lady. she's
in here somewhere. watch
me careful now. I
got a feeling about you. keep
your eye on the black lady. she's
in here somewhere. got
a feeling about you. you
got an intelligent face. you

say your name was Mark? O,
you didn't say? musta been thinkin
bout somebody else. so
what's what?

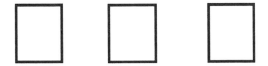

nice try. come on, ain't gonna quit. shit,
we just gettin started. third
time's a charm. uh

o, got

to go. later, Mark, catch you on the flip
flop.

BAND

in this ghost town, any spade
can con his way
into any nightclub
just by *being* black
and at the back door
claiming,

    I'm with the band.

just like that.
any nigger can con his way
like slippin between the spokes
of the wheel of fortune
known as the west
where claims are staked.
names untaken.
second starts given.
pasts forgiven.
between the spokes of the wheel
of where
we be livin.

drinkin in
the landscape.

    these mountains are something else, bro,
    and something else
    is good enough.

drinkin in the land of
not opportunity,
but at best, belief.
at worst, desperation. but

the doors open up for us at night,
when the lights collapse on the crackers
and the sun fucks up
their empire's cons
piracy.

      we breathe.

              respire.

deep.

inside smoke-filled lounges and lungs
of the western recesses and excesses
where race carnivals take place
under cover charges
and of darkness:

      the Paramount.
      the Penthouse.
      the Taj Mahal.
      the Cave.
      the Commodore.
      the Colonial. where

cash crashes down doors
and crackers act
ually inter
act
with niggers slingin slack cash
on a Saturday night. slick
as our music flickers
through the turnstiles

      of theatres
      and booze cans

and after hours joints
and nightclubs
the hub of

darktown
at
Strathcona's
corners,
all the way down
to the intersection of Hastings and Main.

no Negro could really entertain
fantasies of fortune.
how could any even great pretender
get his white hopes up?
about luck
in love
or happenstance.
drunk before the band
that plays our music good enough. it's enough
that the circuit spins the big acts north enough

to Vancouver a
cross the border

        (always an iffy prospect
        like diggin for gold
        or other shades
        of Negro).

blue notes fall
like leaves across roots
that speculate their darkening way
into the truth.

and the fog rolls in

past the docks
and the cop shop
and the steam clock
and takes its time
to intoxicate our section of the city inside. inside,

blues
just
slays
souls. just so

damn
much
cooler
than
Vancouver
asphalt. tar

and feather blues
like truest birds
called home to roost.

you

can get into
any nightclub
in Vancouver
just by *being* black
and at the back door
claiming,

> *I'm with the band.*

EVENING AT THE COLONIAL

in the way of all block
busters, in the way of all casting
calls, in the way of all opening
credits, in the way of names in lights,
we take our seats. Cecil B. DeMille flicks
his tricks of technicolor at me. reels us
in his not-so-on-location direction. his light
forming a film. I and my

homeboys take our seats
in the front row to watch Heston desegregate Egypt.
the usher shouts, 'down in front, darkie!' when my partner
stands up at the sight of those Nubians. sits back down.
stage-whispers to us, 'what the fuck is a Nubian? look like *your*
monkey-asses to me.' cracks us up. but we settle down. sink in

to the thick of the plot. munching on pop
corn and jujubes. crunching
the ice cubes in our drinks. talking back to the screen:
'watch out, Moses! dude's tryna jack you for your grip!'
a theatre full of white folks utter at once,
hoarsely, politely, and quietly,
'ssssssssssssssssshhhhhhhhhhhhhhh!'
like steam let out of a clock. Heston parts

the Red Sea, but it ain't so special. and man,
I'm bored. look to my right and Fuller is rapt. to
my left, Drew is absorbed. just steady popping corn
into his mouth. but man, I'm bored. lean

my head back, look up, up, up.
behold the projector's shaft of light streaming
out past the balcony, solid.
shape carved out
by bits of drifting dust. at least,
that's what I figure.

JAMB

climb
in
to
the
top
of
the
stairs.
top
of
the
stairs   hard to find the real deal up hear.
got   to
the   find
down   the
home   real
sound.   deal
         up
         hear.

slike predicting the weather whether a club on any given night's
                gone get the music right. you pay for it with the sole
of your ears and your whole. and on every given night the do
                        or takes its take of the low
rollers of Negro Vancouver. the low ballers who eye the cover and size

                up
                if
                it's
                gone
                be
                on

it
to
night.

your skin is your ID. you are what you wear.
you're your ear. so what you starin
at, Jack? punk best to back
the fuck up. got me

a razor and a flask of lightning-white rupture
tucked in the folds of my fines. I

glide   on   by.   un

frisked, and up to
the bar. darkly slide
an end to the tender to cover whatever
that drummer is drinkin, the thin brother leanin in
to those breathin drums like they was his lover.
hours make the clock s

ink its hands
into my pockets
in increments. the band blurs me, cymbals sailing, seaming
a blue sealing. my two-tones slide in
to the tw
ine of their seine.
I wash up on the bar, brush the dust off my slur, and gesture
for three shots, for the tender
to pour me a traffic light:

maraschino

gold tequila

crème de menthe

and the ridden spin
        a pin-
striped, pleated
        whorl
to the last swallow and final
        call. feeling hollow
as polite applause for bad magic. anchored and shot.
        glassy. assed out and,
man, immersed
        in thoughts of a lone
                one
                room
whole.   walk
                up

doing one more listlessshuffle.
doing one last pointless jive to nothing. just lifting
a shiftless foot past the jam as the band
breaks   down.
        its gear.

coat check. last check
for whoever might resign to take a sip
of my gaze. a lights up, backfield
Hail Mary attempt
at putting moves
on. no.
so night air.
so lone.
so like a haint.

so one too many shadows even
for my vision. and not even
sudden. my hand hovers for my razor
late. one blinking fist breaks

itself against my, 'wait.'
and lip lisps blood
and lungs leak, 'uh'
and ear stands under, 'nigger'
and ground
and down
and a shuffled deck of my head
in the alley
of the shadow
of my shallow
ness of breath.

face cruxed in
to the very mask of cuss.

      some
      one's
      shoes
      shined
      with
      my
      blood
      clatter
      and
      clatter
      and
      gradually
      shush

as a hex inevitably settles into the langour of ruin.

CROOKED BLUES

a
lone buoy, beached
in a rent-by-the-day. seein
the bones bleachin, fleshin
up
like this Pacific
wrappin
it
self in
to
these foot
prints, rinsing.
starfish.
anemones.
pools.
port sided
and derided. in

       the flesh. lasting four un
              storied centuries. in the sea breathing
      backwards, up
              side down and free. dreaming, bobbing,
      and we've
          ing.

helix of his ear catching
the rhythm. glasses catching
other glasses. hands open like holsters.
awake. temperate baptism.
an eye that simmers
in the sight of any enemy. stare you in
to sewering the cue. just staring, just chewing on a tooth

pick.
ain't no God
damned Moses
come to this here parting of sorrows.
ain't no flock, no con
gregation. ain't got
nothing in these parts, this neck
of the woods.

ain't no God
damned Moses come.
no shepherd
to tread
water. ain't no
one wringing bread or roses
from the pavement. ain't no past
oral poems. ain't no wake of blues. ain't no
mother wit to take the weight
of being take your pick of names.

ain't no God
damned Moses comin. no
ancient Greek lucky breaks, no laurel
wreathes for Negroes. no
deus ex machina. no
fields of satyrs, nymphs, or centres. half
man, half. no
image worth a damn, God. no
door through this epidermis. no
image worth a sucking stone. no
nothing worth a palmed snake.
withering visuals. fake. rolling
the cue a
cross the table
in measure. this game. this cue. wooden. not
the cross, not

the ankh, not
the clock, but
the

CR OO K

hustle on; breakin; fifty bones on the table; eyes cuttin side; ways; spheres
clackin; I; spookin; spoken; takin; this cracker for ten blue tokens; frocked
proper; English; on it; side; Boston block cocked; corner pocket; exact;
pocketing; cash locked; sucker licked; one; two; eye; in; tight;

and so;
let it be broke.

THE BASS

knew this dude once went by the name of Duke
used to walk these here streets corner to corner, sure as you're born,
carrying a big ol bass fiddle case. yass, you heard me.
chump lugged it into restaurants, on buses, jammed it
through the doors of friends' apartments—you get the picture. nigger

couldn't play a lick. word was,
Duke ain't no musician, so what heavy burden
he be hiding in that case? folks in Strathcona
got to gossiping and meditating all kinds of theory as to what
he was packing.

> contraband
> guns
> drugs
> booze
> dead PMs
> poems
> roses
> gold
> who

could know? but we all
had our angle. brother

built a rep as a recluse, an eccentric, a gangster,
a black bard bid to sing. everyone axed him;
he never conceded an answer. just smiled
and lugged that case another block, hitch-hiking
off its sphinx-like vibe. its minor-key mystery.
leaving a trail of gossip. case on him like a tail on a snake,
a shell on a snail. leaving a spit-wet wake
of speculation. but I been around the block

enough times to know, course,

ain't nothing in that case and never was.
fool started something he couldn't finish, trying to wear intrigue
like tweed. can still see him hobbling up the street,
case too big to walk straight, too empty to open up.

THE COMMODORE

A.   B.

the beautiful ones don't stand in line	y'hear? the blues man Johnny Ace
talked the cover down to three for two,	just iced hisself down in Houston. spun
and we're in	his pistol chambers, double
to the cool bluesy splendour	zeroed hisself off into the sunset
of transgression. looking for the coloureds	for the love of some white girl.
to make us women. unfurling at the bar	dreams all blasted out the back
like a sail. hear that?	of his belief, ain't that some shit.
the band's covering Johnny Ace.	but the south is the south and this ain't,
'The Clock.' a tribute, I suppose. hear	so see that blue
what happened? so tragic. so romantic.	eyed
such a shame. you can hear the devotion	beau
in that slow, breathing beat.	ty over there? that one. check it,
I can hear the contrast of his hand	I'm gonna talk to her.
in hers. I can hear it, the way coloureds	step to her. slip
hold us. tight. like something won.	my number in
like that one over there,	to her hand, kiss it, swirl her
the one with his hat	like I was dialing, moving
cocked and that delicious grin.	so I can see us out the corner of my eye in
I just got here and, I swear, let him ask me	the mirror behind the bar. see if I can see
for my number, and we split this joint	from her face if she digs me,
one two	if I got half a chance
stead of	of taking
two ones.	her home.

ALLEY BLUES

no congregation. pasts to shake.
to lose.

no going back. just space to take
up. fools

      running

the place. renting us
ramshackle truths.

          alley blues.

at the terminal

call
for alcohol. in our own

dark
town, night
trips. falls
on us

      down

in what
always. is

        darktown.

DIAMOND

I belong irreducibly to my time.

—Frantz Fanon

I had passed through a quarter century, and finally my vision was going. I blamed it on reading. There were signs at the university warning you about everything from date rape to late capitalism, but nothing that said anything about reading yourself blind. I was trying to get used to the glasses, but they caused the worst sort of nightmares from the very start. My optometrist claimed it was a normal phenomenon as one gets used to a prescription. At the end of the day there were times I was rendered so dizzy and in such pain that I threw up.

But while reading I came to learn the names of all nine Muses: Calliope, Clio, Erato, Euterpe, Melpomene, Polyhymnia, Terpsichore, Thalia, and Urania. I also learned about the Scylla and Charybdis, which sounded familiar when I heard them mentioned in lecture. I realized my mom had told me about the sea monster and the whirlpool when I was a little kid. She'd turned the old myth into a children's bedtime story.

All my friends when I was a kid were mixed like me. Our parents were interracial couples, as they say, and us Civil Rights babies, I guess. Back in those days, the mixed couples stuck together. It was still freaky as hell in the early seventies, I imagine, to see a black man and a white woman pushing a pram with a nappy-headed kid flaunting its golden skin to the world. Brazen. Birds of a feather, as they say.

So the mixed couples flocked together playing cards, and us, their children, fought over who got to play Lando Calrissian in the backyard.

I once saw my mother cuss out a young white hippie woman. The woman was walking up the street towards us with her mixed baby. Baby had little golden dreads growing out like caterpillar fern tendrils. My mom, who don't know from dreads, castigated the woman something fierce, saying, 'When I married a black man I made damn sure I knew how to comb a black child's head. You have no excuse for letting that poor child walk around, head all knotted up. Are you out of your mind?' In Mom's day, you had to fight tooth and nail for every inch of respect. They were looking for excuses and you best not be giving them any.

I came to learn the names of all three Furies, too: Alecto, Megaera, Tisiphone.

●

I bumped into one of those old friends, mixed progeny, a good buddy of mine I had kept up with only through the odd encounter and mostly rumour. He lived in the sticks now, in Delta, apparently. His name was Cameron, and he had always been a smart and unusual guy. Last I'd heard he was fronting a Marxist punk rock band called Hammer and Sickle Cell Anemia, and dating a white girl who played bass in an all-girl hardcore band. But when I walked into A&B Sound, there he was, the picture of hip hop.

We soul shook.

'Sup? I ain't seen you in ages, nigga! Whatcha bin doin'?'

I filled him in, we caught up a bit. Turns out he was a DJ now, had a gig coming up at The Quarter. He passed me a handbill with a slick and dizzyingly cartoonish design. Said,

Featuring DJ T-Rope, N.W.N. (Niggas With Négritude), DJ Osiris, Grand Master Narrative and the Tenuous Ten, and DJ Parataxis

'Which one is you?'

'I'm DJ Osiris. I know, there's one in every city in North America, but whatcha gone do. Sounds too cool!'

'Osiris. The god, right?'

'Dass right. Pan-Africanism, home, that's where I'm coming from these days. The Afrocentric shit. The funky dialectic. You get to study much of our own stuff up at that school?'

'No. None at all.' It was true. I felt embarrassed, here in the presence of Osiris, about how little I knew of Africa.

'Yeah, well, it wasn't until I *left* school that I started to learn things. Like Plato and Aristotle and those motherfuckers stole all their shit from Egypt. A thief culture, that's what the West is. Everything that ain't nailed down, they take. Check it.' He rifled through his backpack and produced a book with an amateurish graphic of a pyramid on the cover. 'I'm learning to read hiero-glyphics, man. That's the kind of cultural shit I'll get into in my MCing, if I ever get some money together. Right now I'm just DJing, but I'm trying to polish my voice, my delivery. You know, get the skills up. I need to get paid, is what I need. Got ta get paid, is what I got ta get.'

We stared at each other for a bit. I didn't remember him ever talking like this when we were kids, this accent.

'Well, I'll see you later. . . .' I hesitated, not sure if I was supposed to call him Cameron or Osiris. 'I'll try to check out your show.'

'Later,' said my new old friend, and we knocked fists, and he left.

●

As soon as I got to the club I realized I'd left my ID at home. I was always doing this. The pants I usually wore out to clubs didn't have a back pocket, so I would take my money out of my wallet, put it in my front pocket, and leave the wallet at home. Half the time it wouldn't occur to me to bring my ID, or that I'd get carded at twenty-five. When I arrived, the doorman was propped up on a wobbly stool, wobbling and counting the heads streaming by with a little metal clicker.

'ID,' he said to me, and only me, even though the three girls ahead couldn't've been a day over fifteen.

'I left my ID at home. Look, man, I'm twenty-five years old.'

'I need to see some ID.' He didn't even look me in the eye. More probable minors breezed by while he arbitrarily singled me out.

'Listen, I really am twenty-five. I can prove it. Would an eighteen-year-old know all nine Muses? There's Calliope, Clio, Erato, Euterpe, Mel-pomene. . . .'

He turned and looked at me. 'What the fuck are you talking about?'

'The Muses. You know, the ancient Greek goddesses of the arts, the daughters of Zeus and Mnemosyne, the . . .'

He stood up, and his stool fell over. He was easily six inches taller than me, a face as blank as paper. 'Are you fucking with me, you piece of shit?'

'No, man, I'm trying to prove to you that I'm over eighteen. I'm studying Brecht. I know who Devo are. I owned a Rubik's Cube. I can locate a clitoris on a woman. What more evidence do you need?'

Before he could pull my arms off, Osiris peeped his head out of the front door and saved me. 'Nigga, getchyo ass in here. My set's coming up.' And to the doorman, a simple 'He's with me' even absolved me of the cover.

●

It was like stepping inside a rattle: the dancers in their gear, the players laying back, the homegirls hip-shaking. We skirted the floor, bought pints at the bar, and then made our way to a little stage up against the back wall. The platform was surrounded by people jackin it up. The current DJ was in position before the wheels, needles centripetal on the vinyl. I marvelled that this place was so thick with sound you had to wade through it, and all that sound passed through a tiny piece of diamond on the end of a needle, on the end of an arm, on a turntable, on a table, on this stage. Some dude leaning against the wall said to Osiris, 'You up next, O.'

'They just trying different people out tonight,' Osiris said to me. 'Five or six motherfuckers are here. Comin from all over. . . .'

Osiris's voice trailed off. He became distracted by the current DJ's cutting. A craftsman observing a colleague, I observed. I could tell O was nervous and probably hadn't been doing this long. He turned away while the current DJ grooved, and started stretching like a man up to bat. He was talking at me a mile a minute, sort of rambling.

'All sorts of shit kept from us. All sorts of shit. Bitch-ass white dude asked me today why if Africans are so into the drum, the talking drum and all that shit, why there are so few rock drummers who are black? *Maybe cause we don't get down to that Geddy Lee-Rush-stadium rock shit, motherfucker.* Ain't like my dad was beating bongos at the dinner table, peckerwood. White people in this city are so backward. Can't even get their racism right. Technology is our thing, why ain't it? I don't play no goddamn drums. I *program* the fuckin hell outta shit, though. Why we gotta be so *earthy*? Stupid backwater crackers. You know, they ain't cornered the market on technology. Hell, no. Every time you stuck at a red light bitchin bout, "I'm gonna be late for work," just think, a black man's shit is fucking you up. Brother named Garrett Augustus Morgan invented the motherfuckin traffic lights, man.'

'I didn't know that. . . .' I could feel a headache coming on. I touched my temples with my fingers and rubbed them in a circular motion.

'Of course you didn't know that. Ever wonder why they're red, yellow, and green? Colours of the Ethiopian flag, man. Garrett Augustus Morgan was a righteous inventing motherfucker. Think they want you to know shit like that? Naw, go bang a fuckin drum, jungle bunny. Don't think about doing anything that'll last longer than a few vibrations in the air. Anyway, whatever. Say, tell me some shit you're learnin about at school, home. Take my mind off this. I'm stressed out up here. Shit, this place is packed.'

I started to tell him about how I'd been doing some reading on my own, stuff about blacks in west coast history, the gold rush days, the first influx of us, but the music was so loud it seemed like my voice was being whisked away the moment it left my mouth. I could barely hear my own words, except as they vibrated inside my head. The club boomed. It felt like a giant was picking up the club and dropping on the ground over and over again in four four time. Squeals of synth and sampled horn gasped at me humanly, unbearably. My mind balked. My vision crumpled. I held onto a column and downed my beer. A migraine was clearly arising. 'The Egyptians invented beer,' I heard a voice say, but it wasn't DJ Osiris; he was already in front of the turntables for his set.

He must've hit the right nerve; there was a floor rush as soon as his first few beats broke out. Bodies started bobbing and bearing into me on all sides. I was swept out onto the floor. The bass buzzed in my skull, vibrated up inside my teeth. A speaker was just above my head; I could feel wind emanating from the cones. My heart paradiddled. There was just the pulse and ebb of each boom of bass and residual crack of manufactured snare:

WOOM BOOM CRACK

WOOM BOOM CRACK

In succession, cessation, succession, my friend's Afrocentric cut flowed like blood from the speaker above me, wailing, a voice chopped, saying, sort of singing,

New Af ri ca—
Ne w Afri ca—
New Af rica at tackin ya

and the boom bloomed into the next subsequent crack like I imagined a round from a Kalashnikov would sound. My eyes tore open with water. Through each succession of blur, the darkness, the spinning, the lights, the smoke, the colliding, the limbs, the dreads, the glasses, the tears, the drink, the woom, the boom, the crack, I saw the edges of the room, a box beneath the ground, a basement with concrete walls, with exposed pipes, with a vague floor on which white kids spun like dreidels, breaking, locking, popping, windmilling, spinning counter-clockwise.

And his hands, brass, curved into each title of vinyl as he replaced one record, then another, holding up the vibe, straddling ecstasy and vengeance, pulling back tracks, cutting, retracing steps, thefts. I could barely see the vinyl spinning on the steel through what felt like blood welling behind my bruised eyes. There was glitter.

He lifted a record up from its place on the turntable, holding it gently with both hands as if it were the most fragile and precious thing he'd ever touched. The deafening roar of time rushed by as through a door the size of a year and tore into sediment. Tears ran down my face, chest, soaked me, tugged at my ankles like a current. I reached out to steady myself. Everything, everyone, was moving, bouncing up and down. Shadows teemed. Just then, my glasses were swept off my face in a single, sharp, staggering blow.

HEAR

I say 'a ways ahead' for in my creole way, fifty feet, fifty yards, fifty metres, is the same thing.
—Claire-Marie Hitchens

RED LIGHT BLUES

it's the colour
they tell you *no* in, in

voking blood perhaps or
fire to keep you, a pack,
at bay. English don't

exist in the cross
walk. here we speak
in pictographs, glyphs, i
cons. X

for tracks that cut you
off from other
sides.

the hand offends me.
the white man eternally gives the go a
head. the hand
that clasps
your sullen undoing
is read.

you could wait a thousand years,
a glacier's day,
for the dotted lines
to sign your right
of way. the right passage
of entrance in
to the right terrain.

when your destination
is the crossing,

how do you know
when you've made it? we,

the strays of the race, the wild
goose chasers, after

rainbows and caul
drons of response
and arrival,

       allegedly
            shelved
                  on the beams
                        of the aurora
                              borealis.

SPORT OF THE KING OF KINGS

how to read the program:

—horse colour
——sex
————age
————place foaled
——————name of sire
———————name of dam
————————name of sire of dam

abbrev. & symbols:

race information:
be—broken equipment
acc—accident
p—placed by judges
I—intersected
©—boxed in
†—hoppled
bl—bled
ch—choked
χ—broke stride

race distance:
m—one mile
n—9/16 mile
s—1 1/16 mile
h—1/2 mile dash
f—5/8 mile dashed
hy—1/2 mile hyphenated
q—1/4 mile quadroonated
– —back to Africa
+—to the crossroads

horse exegesis:
B—bay
Blk—black
C—chestnut
Hy—high yellow
R—roan
W—white
X—negro
Ω—pale

c—colt
f—filly
g—gelding
h—horse
m—mare
r—ridgling
s—spayed
t—crossed

who got the copyright
on the King James thing?

alphabetized mind,
omega nigga.
alphabetized, mined
down to a chiastic claim.

X

marks the stain
of Cain of Cain of Cain
but who got the copyright
on the King James thang?

rhyme me up a river
or a name. me? a lame-
horse better, at the wicket
staking claims.

ripping up washed up
tickets to easy street. tripping
steps on brassy sand. picking
through the pro
gram for a hint
like an ibis
on the hunt
for in
sects, for
another day.

beak
in the banks.
beak
in the beach breaks.
skanking on

the moon's off
beats. like Bob

Marley with the mic
in his palm like
the sword of the righteous, swingin,
                    " 'until
                        the
                        phil
            osophy which holds one race superior and another
                inferior is finally and permanently discredited
                        and
                        aband
                        oned,
                        every
                        where
                        is
                        war

war up north

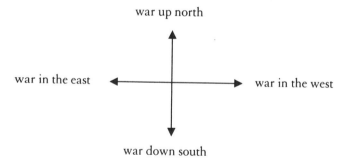

war in the east   war in the west

war down south

war
war
rumours of
war." '

(who got the copy-
right?) Marley fights

them down

down with the sword of his mouth
mouth
and his tongue of fire. fire
of eye. eye
of dread. dread
of tendril. on
high. high
on. bliss
of brass. fire
come. tongue
fire. earth
of kiln. lap
of sky. I
and
I

sometimes feel
like a motherless tongue
berthed
tied
as noosed as Judas
sold down the river of time.

still

I sharpen my spear like a cue
and break, tidal. blacks
(they say)
are good at pool:
something to do
with ancient Egyptian

or Islamic geometry?
the divinity of math, the afro
centric, concentric like
360°
like a clock
like a track
like a poem?

or maybe just something to do

with rolling and gathering
no moss
rolling and gathering
no Moses
rolling along
collecting no lichen
rolling along
like Hendrix covering Dylan
likening—

                            ' "how does it *feel*
to be on your own

                [home

land]?" '

someday my ship will come in
someday our shining black prince will come
numbers running
to the end, and up
ending diadems, in
a black beret, blasting off,
offing cops, bucking rounds,
bucking down contending clowns
on the march like Mao,

all on the long long shot to pay off, down
to back
the exact
mount.

sages of the race
track
leaf through pages of the pro
gram
like selecters in a dancehall.
stylin like Solomon.
'I like such-and-such,' and
'so-and-so looks good in the seventh.'
one of the wisest of the wise
looking comely
scrutinizes
the racing form.
his fighting chances
these choices:

THE SUN DOWNS
December 31, 1999

7TH RACE
Warm-up Cloth—blue   Purse—you

Blue   BLANK EPOCHS

1
          W g 6 (East) Pox Vopuli—HBC Rainbow—Blanket Statement

Blue   KNIGHT VISION

2
          C c 2 (West) Infrared—Pale Rider—Clint Westwood

Blue   GRAVE FORECAST

3   Blk h 4 (North) Caste O' Thousands—Flash Flood—100% Chance Of Rein

Blue   STONE HARVEST

4 Ω h 6 (South) Baron Samedi—Grim Reaper—Conqueror

(All others scratched in the final race.)

TIDE

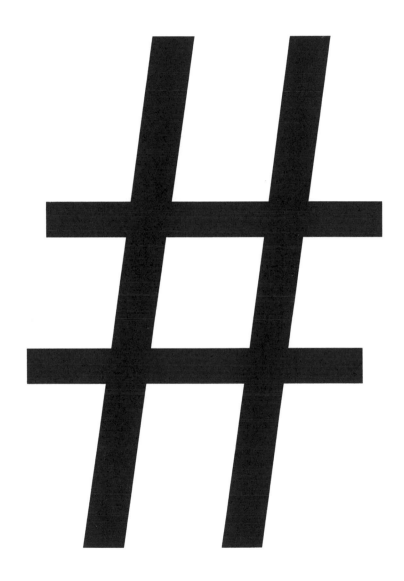

WAX

7

77

777

7777

77777

777777

BABYLON SLIM'S SONG

I drawl along the street bumpin
'Baby That's Backatchya' on my walkman. got
a Ph.D. in Black English, studied under Dr. Dre.
so I book

down to meet my man
on the corner, in the crook
of this herded tin-ankh town
north of nowhere, Babylon
late. on CPT. coloured people's time.
we greet by
knocking fists,
knocking for,
knocking at
the gates of straight-no-chaser,
new-world-order,
blue-lipped, stone-cold
African't
blues. so *we* book

past the Chinese herbalist,
past the Native prestidigitist,
past the Latin sidewalk symphonist
hawking his version of 'Against All Odds.'
and I ain't got no change.
we threadbare, me and my bro,
my shadow. west coasting
where blacks be more rarely seen
than a sasquatch's back teeth. but *I* see

all this race shit going down.
nothing gets past
this last

inheritor
of all sideshows
and imported minstrel moans.
the heir to the King of the Sidekicks' ottoman throne. shit,

you'd think this was something new
or something. hell, no. no new
thing under the aurora borealis.
no will o' the whip,
no amount o' ocean going
gonna make this shit stop.
we stuck with it. fuck,

you'd think this was something new
or something. white boys callin
each otha 'nigga'—maybe that's new.
but mostly SOS. same old shit. ever

wonder why I so loudly
signify? so you know
these streets be
mine
mine
mine. even the sky
and that there arc
of seven colours
licking the mountains
like a snake fixing to take
a couple steps
into a toad's nest. 'be blessed,'

I hear that old street preacher say
to no one in particular.
before
before
before

he fixes his fucked up baby browns on me,
old, corny, crazy, preachin-in-my-face, breathin-boozy-fire-and-woozy-
inebriations-of-a-caged-bird-singin, grey-dreadlock-havin, NDP-votin,
old-age-pension-spendin fool
says to *me*,
Babylon Slim,
and I quote:

    'you,
    my young brother,
    will never understand
    what it *really* means
    to be black. I
    was raised down south
    before all this bullshit
    before
    before
    before
    and you ain't never gonna understand,
    with your X paraphernalia
    and your gangsta jive
    how you coulda been strung up
    for lookin at an ofay sideways
    how you coulda
    before
    how you coulda
    before
    before we did the burnin down,
    they did the burnin up. get it,
    kid?' says this to *me*. mother

fucker. but shit.
it's plain as day.
old nigga
got the same hard-on as me
for those same fucking blue as god-knows-what
mountains.

TO

Selassie Eye a run
the dance floor. a rum
from back home. open closed
like strobes. the national

lines and the parallel
points of compass and light. the times.

and Selassie Eye a run
the floor. a rum
from back home. open
and closed. like globes

halved, hemisphered, creoled, covered,
and someday wholed. I
see Selassie in
between the movers. holy
living man. in
a sackcloth tam and two
fingers to
the sky barnacled with lights wired in time
to the one one two. holy

living man. a run
the place. a one
from back home. open

and closed.

TWO TURN

●

whose world this is? two speakers exhaling helically a camel's eye's worth
of stacked

● ●

dub plates. acetate. sharp as a chorus of coral. wreckin ship. scratches
whistlin,

● ● ● ●

'Bronx'. rocks'. locks'. blacks'. stocks'.' cracking. transposition. canon

● ● ● ● ● ● ●

got a brand new bang. node I'm sayin? after)centric)styling

● ● ● ● ● ● ● ● ● ● ●

from(to(back slid)e)liding mix(ingcry(ing, 'what's my

● ● ● ● ● ● ● ● ● ● ● ● ● ● ● ● ●

mother? fuckin? name?'

● ●

PILLAR

'The Negro's tale is a poignant one and it will never be told in full. Most of the first people who immigrated to Salt Spring wished to forget their past. Here they found the freedom they had never known in their own land. Their descendants, who live on Salt Spring Island today, concur in their forebear's preference. They wisely do not want to look back.'

—Bea Hamilton, *Salt Spring Island* (1969)

up the I, suckers, reach
for the sky. cause this is a hold
up, and I
've finally come
for what's mine:

'The first settlers of Salt Spring Island were Negroes and came as early as 1857 (9?), seeking liberty and freedom from discrimination. Family names of these earliest settlers were

[Buckner   Robinson
      Curtis   Isaac
          Davis   Wall
                  Whims
          Spotts   Jones
      Shore   Lester
Robertson   Thompson].'

—Richard Mouat Toynbee, *Snapshots of Early Salt Spring* (1969)

+

Howard Estes (bought himself with $ from California gold prospectin), and his wife
Hannah Estes, and their son
Jackson Estes, and their daughter . . .

Sylvia Estes		Sylvia Stark
+ Louis Stark	x	Louis Stark
Sylvia Stark		Willis Stark

'Panthers and wolves in those days swarmed on the island and
prevented any attempt at keeping cattle or sheep. One man [Willis]
relates how he and his father [Louis] shot nine panthers between
them within a few weeks one autumn, and the howling of wolves
was a constant source of disturbance at nights.'
        —Reverend E.F. Wilson, *Salt Spring Island, 1895*

now.
don't be looking for no black folks there
now.
ain't but half a handful there, at press.
all moved to Victoria. Vancouver. the States. wherever. what you ex
pect from people
got names like 'Whims'?

THE UNBROKEN YELLOW

round the fire, ringed, telling
ghost tales. placing
another limb of drift
wood. another plank
planed by the sea. wondering

which one of the flames
leaps from my piece of wood.

BLUER BLUES

the water in
which you wade
is holy. drowning

      under

the mountains and their wishful blue, where the gods live.
where the birds hang. fore they turn
back, looking.

          glass
          case: please break
              in case of caste

discrimination. and if one more some
body asks me where I'm from today
I'm gonna offer,

          'out there in that ocean
          where you left me
          when you drifted away. I got no'

better response. see, as kids we spun
the globe closing
our eyes, going,

          'here
          gonna be my home.' globe rolling
          on a plastic axis,

finding our little digits dis
appointedly in the middle
of the ocean. later and I'm still ambiv

alently coloured and liv
ing in Xanada,
trying to spell and accent *Santeria* and *Aime Cesaire,*
trying to prounounce *houngan*, trying to try, trying to care,
whispering red into the embers, fading, late. CPT. trying
to keep my
self smouldering, thinking,

'Halfrican'

at others in cafés, the talented
tenth of a percent, trying
to keep anchored,
above the line, to keep a language
living, envying
patois or nation
language, or anything, the Asians.
trying truly to truly try,
trying to keep the third world in mind,
trying to riot,
trying to buy it,
trying to put it together and get it undone. clocks set at set trip
on some nigger mumbling mumbling chicken blood, flicking
chicken blood at the white page, spelling, dialing, dilating
the accent, eccent, afrocent, ricity, outward, goose-stepping still is
goose stepping even done to call and response, trying to call
Amiri Baraka Leroi Jones in my time of casting away stones
and gathering together, some
time after and above Watts, or when
ever when
ever.

meeting on the corner
a voice without a body.

'even echoes got echoes. yo. in the mixture, in history. à la
Ali. mess with me and we'll be gettin it on like Frantz
Fanon. because I'm pretty. teach you the Ten Point
Program the hard way. with revisions too. point eleven:
just leave me alone.'

Lou Reed
on the tape deck,
Ishmael Reed
in his black leather jacket pocket,
in the back seat with Debbie counting
her freckles and the fractions and the nature
of white rhythmlessness, meaning she's late,
and he's thinking, *ain't gonna be one gram of African*
in that child, dying, drowning
in those eyes, and it's unspeakable,
how much the pieces mean, doing
long division, spreading
out and creating a little love,
which is what
the world needs now, as they say, or something
close enough. the almost off

spring sings. the on-the-head-of-a-needle Coulda-Been
will take us home. softly now. musing.

                    'spectrum comes through re
                    fraction, Damballah and Ayida Wedo
                    copulating. circling. staff to myth;
                    sticks to getting; stoned to tripping; it's
                    all. no. good. spinning. Southern
                    Comfort; west coast ease. sugar
                    and shit, like love. pressing play
                    on my tongue
                    like a snake. listening.
                    seeing. with it's tongue. re

winding the magnetism of poles
making the lights dance like night
club strobes. running. north. loving seeing
breath making solid the cold.
a seen soul. sold. getting
a decent day's pay. getting
to heaven, which was what
I was after, after
all. over
the rainbow, sevenly shaded
blue, exact hue
of an already sky.'

49TH PARALLEL PSALM

sinking Zion's song
into a stranger's land.
sing Zion signified
among the other others.
sing bitter-sweet science
in back alleys like Ali
over colourless hopes.
sinking Zion's song
in the west.

in the nightclub with
all the other others
breaking I contact with the brothers
in track suits
and timber boots.
white b-boy
at the turntables
cuttin up the track,
cuttin on the word (((n i g g a))) on the
                    cross
                    cross
                    fader.

downtown in the Chameleon Lounge,
Sonar, the Starfish Room,
the Commodore or
Granville Seven.
admit one point seven
million
boxed by these mountains.
on the ropes.

snow-white screams of

back where you came from

you framed in
the cold silver light
of satellites and beams
that screen but can't see
the borders from space.
so cold
over the rainbow.
the cinematography casts the line,
the right light,
keepin it
reel.

dancing with Snow White
to the sampled gunshots.
she flicks her hair like super eight film
at the edit.
cut. dreads

don't lock
or pop
or break
but black
star line us back, rewind us
to Zion's song.
synching to dancehall
of mirrors. the sister in
red, gold, green. the mirror
globes glitter like moons.
gold skin glistenin.
Malcolm said we auriferous.
can't speak for the speakers, but she,
I later learn, flew in from

(((E t h i o p i a)))
on a silver wing.
sinking
Zion's song into a stranger's land.
we librate

cross the floors.
cross all that glitters.
cross the subliminal urban stars.
treading water,
tracks,
head taxes.
to get, hear.
to wear here.
to where we be
subliminal

     ain't but ten black people in all of be see

but we can't count
on the crackers,
and they can't seem to sense us.
claiming the numbers
is against us.

black like wax tracks.
free-at-last markets. black
like the invisible hand pans.
East Van represent.
blackness all in my cipher,
living on the weals of steal—

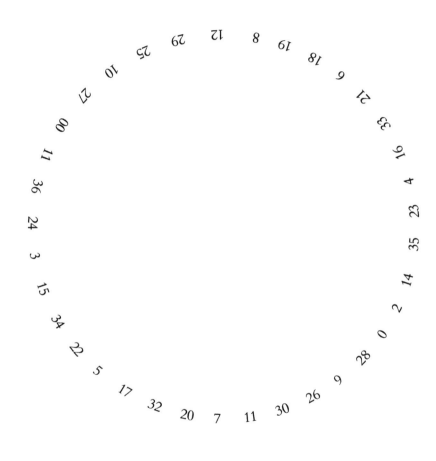

12

11   1

10   2

9   3

8   4

7   5

6

ebbing on into the promissory land on the eagle's left wing.
the wheel of the plane scratches a runway song
broken north.
above ground railways.
runaway trains of thought.
north for the winter.
every colour of the rain.
panning for amber in the traffic,
at the flood gates,
at the centre Legba spins
on his one good leg
and blows the whistle.
like a reed or tenor
so tender
in its ravages.
like Bird Parker
in a loop,
a swoop.
waving.
hitch-hiking.
directing accident after
accident after
the fact.
I in the cross
walk
colliding.
waiting for the light to turn

                                    red

                            black

                    or green.

synching Zion's song analog.
diasporic digits strum the striations.

leaf through pages of moraine.
the motion of Moses' hands.
I imagine
borders giving way just the same
as a read sea.

a read me.
a people of colour.
digital leaves
tryina keep it real

> *a cappella*
> *aurora borealis*
> *pax Britannica*
> *curriculum vitae*
> *vox Africana*

skin between,
but there,
I hear,
the breath we draw before the next line

is singing

WAYDE COMPTON has been
published in numerous literary
magazines. He was born in
Vancouver, where he still lives,
and is a student and teaching
assistant at Simon Fraser
University.